THIS SOLDIER'S FORTUNE

THE TRIALS AND TRIUMPHS OF A POLISH SOLDIER IN WWII

Connor Court Publishing
Ballan, Australia

Published in 2010 by Connor Court Publishing Pty Ltd

Copyright © Zygmunt Tratkiewicz, 2010
Not to be reproduced without permission of the Copyright holder.
All rights reserved

ISBN: 978-1-921421-33-4

Connor Court Publishing Pty Ltd
PO Box 1
Ballan VIC 3342
Phone (03) 9005 9167
Fax (03) 5303 0960
sales@connorcourt.com
www.connorcourt.com

Printed in Australia
Cover designed by Brigid Cappello

TABLE OF CONTENTS

	Introduction	1
1	Humble Beginnings	3
2	Growing Up	7
3	Further Studies	12
4	Military Life	16
5	War Erupts	20
6	Retreat	32
7	Hungary	45
8	Into Captivity	53
9	Germany	67
10	Stalag V111B	74
11	Guttenberg	77
12	Meddersheim	89
13	Rebellion	104
14	Liberation	109
15	The Polish Brigade	117
16	Italy	120
17	Monte Cassino	123
18	Attack on the Monastery	128
19	My Fighting is Over	132
20	My New Life	137

Introduction

A person will experience many challenges, adventures and changes throughout their life. Some of these experiences will be bad, with a few of these reaching the point of total despair or even sheer terror, or they may feel and become soul destroying. Many more will be ambivalent and fade into the other memories of life. Then there will be the good experiences, some of which will be more than pleasant and are capable of bringing the person to tears from the pleasure and contentment they provide. Some experiences will seem more important because of what the person has lived through, what they may have done or what they may have witnessed.

Most people will never come to understand or achieve the heights of which they are capable or what they can and will do when they see no other option. They may never come to understand what they could withstand and the pain and suffering that they can endure.

Even now, in the ninety-third year of my life, I find that such events and experiences are still indelibly printed in my psyche. They have remained both explicit and graphic and will continue to be with me for the rest of my life.

This story covers just one of the important journeys of my life. It has been written to give my growing family and my friends an insight into a private part of me. It happened many years ago but I can still remember it as if it was yesterday.

1

Humble Beginnings

I was born on the 5th of November 1915 to Jozef and Agnieszka Tratkiewicz. The First World War was still in progress throughout Europe. I am the fourth of their nine children, having three sisters and five brothers.

My birthplace was Zwola, a small farming village in Poland. Our family survived the anguish and hardships and occupation of WW1 but I was only a young child so I have no memories of those years. In this war, Poland was once again invaded and occupied by Germany and its allies. These same peoples were to invade and occupy my country again nearly twenty-four years later. This time I was to play a part in the war against them and then rejoice in their ultimate defeat. As it turned out, this was only part of Poland's eventual problem because the Russians, who came as liberators, stayed after the war to occupy the country for another forty-five years. This communist occupation and repression created much misery to a proud nation and its people. It was only after the Russians had gone and communism had crumbled to reveal what it really was, that the Poles could rebuild their pride as well as their country.

The history of Poland is that for centuries it has

been regularly invaded and occupied by the Germans and Austrians from the west or the Russians from the east. Somehow, the Poles have always managed to survive. In its time Poland had also been a superpower, occupying large areas of Europe from what is now the Ukraine and Belarus to the east, the Baltic States with its border stretching from the Black Sea to the Baltic Sea. Indeed, Poland's borders have waxed and waned often over centuries depending at times on its own power and strength and at other times on the desires and political wants of its more powerful neighbours.

The world that I was born into was ever so different to the world that exists today (in the year 2009). In Zwola, life was still based on a feudal system and remained quite insular. Little had changed from the way of life that existed prior to WW1, where hard work was the norm, life's luxuries were few and only a small number of people ever travelled any great distances. Generally, people lived, worked, married, raised their children and then died within the communities into which they were born.

In many ways life in 1915 was harsh by today's standards. Imagine what your life would be like without today's everyday necessities such as electricity for light, heating and cooking, radio and television for news and entertainment, hot and cold running water for cooking and washing, family motor cars and passenger aeroplanes for travel, computers and the thousands of other little luxuries that you now take for granted. There was no electricity in Zwola or indeed in many parts of rural Poland. Running hot and cold water would have been an absolute treat. There were some cars but there were no roads, particularly outside major cities and towns. In fact I was not to see my first car until I was in my teens. Many of the other things that make today's living and working easier and better had not yet even been conceived in the minds of their eventual creators.

The system of living that prevailed was one of total involvement within the family and the small community in which the Tratkiewicz family lived. From the time I was able to do anything beyond play, I was assigned chores around the farm. Every member of the family had a role to fulfill and there were no exceptions. My early recollections are that there were chickens and ducks to feed, eggs to collect, bird coops and roosts to clean out, water to be brought in from the outside well and wood for the stove to be collected and stacked. I was then also responsible for helping my brothers and sisters with their jobs. My role within the family changed and expanded as I grew. I gained experience in farm work and became stronger, so I was assigned a greater range and harder work. My old chores were passed on to my younger brothers and sisters, who in turn passed them on when the time was right for them to step up.

This is the way that things were within all the other families within our community. There were times when families needed to work together to sow fields and harvest crops. There were no mechanical devices such as tractors or harvesters, so families would help each other when help was needed. The fields were ploughed using a horse pulling a plough together with man's muscle power. All seed planting was done by hand, while crops were harvested with the use of scythes. The crops were allowed to dry and then gathered onto carts using pitchforks. Every farm had their own large vegetable garden that needed constant attention and nurturing. This work relied on brawn and muscle power and was often back breaking. This was what was expected of us and it was all of this hard work that put food on the table and provided a roof over our heads. Everyone had to pull their own weight.

The main escape from work was usually on a Sunday when some members of the family went into the village to attend mass at the church. Poles are a proud people and are still very religious. Every Sunday, the family members who could be spared from farm work would dress in their best clothes and head off to church, with a community get-together afterwards. This provided a welcome relief from farm work and outside these times there were limited opportunities to meet friends or other people from outside the immediate family unit.

My parents, my family, the community in which I lived and grew up, as well as life's large and small experiences, have influenced and shaped my life. I developed my own personal values and beliefs as well as inherited many from my family. Most of these values and beliefs have stayed with me, so far to the age of ninety-three and probably will now until the day I die. As a child or young boy, and then as a young man, growing up in Zwola, I could not begin to imagine what lay before me or what I would experience, or where my life would eventually lead. I also had no conception of how important these beliefs and values would be for the retention of my sanity and providing me with the strength to endure and survive what lay ahead of me.

2

Growing Up

There are many things for which I am grateful to my parents, and education is one of them. They believed that education was essential and ensured that we all received as good an education as was available to us. From this good foundation, most members of my family have made a good fist of their lives either within or outside of farming.

My education began at the local school in Zwola. It was located about a kilometer from the farm. To get to and from school we had no option but to walk. Some other students had to walk further so I was quite fortunate in that regard. When you are young and there is no other alternative you take walking in your stride. During the winter if it wasn't raining it was snowing, so we all either trudged through quagmires that were the roads, or through snow into which we would sometimes sink up to our knees. If we were fortunate, we might be able to hitch a ride on a sleigh or a cart, but such a luxury did not happen very often.

I was a good student right through school, receiving good marks and glowing school reports. However, being good at school didn't save me from duties and chores on the farm. Each morning we rose early to do our chores, have breakfast and then head off for school. When the day's schooling ended we went home to more chores, did our homework, had dinner and then went off to bed. This was the usual routine of life for a boy or teenager living on a farm. This routine rarely changed except when there was no school. Regardless, the farm always had something else which needed doing and quickly ate up any spare time I might have otherwise had. Perhaps this explains why even now I can't sit down without doing anything for any length of time. I still enjoy the opportunity to go out and do something, particularly anything physical, with my hands.

As a toddler I had a good and healthy appetite. I was given the nickname "Fatty" by my family. When I started school the nickname followed me, even though it no longer really applied. Work on the farm saw to that. I did not like the nickname so I was often involved in schoolyard fights. I was able to hold my own on most occasions and eventually the nickname died out. I can remember on at least one occasion I received a good hiding from one of the teachers for being involved in a fight. Schools believed in corporal punishment in those days and I was seen as the aggressor, even if I wasn't the instigator. I, of course, saw the entire matter differently as I was only standing up for myself.

One of the reasons that I was then a little rotund as a young child is my sweet tooth. Sweets and lollies were not readily available but even if they were, I did not have the money to buy any. Pocket money was something unheard of. I still managed to develop a love for the taste of sugar. To keep the household sugar supply out of my reach my mother would suspend the sugar in a bag from the ceiling. This worked at home but as I grew older and supposedly smarter, I was prepared to go to great lengths to satisfy my needs. One of my school friends also had a sweet tooth and often brought a good supply of sugar to school. I made a deal with him to sell him my mathematics book for six blocks of sugar. He gave me the sugar and I handed over my book. As luck would have it, my mother learned of what I had done and this led to trouble for me. Not only did I receive a good hiding but she also gave me the sugar to redeem my book. I was extremely embarrassed by this episode and would not dare to do anything like that again. I had to find more subtle ways of obtaining a supply. To this day I still have the taste for sugar, and any tea or coffee I have must be very sweet. My family describes it as having tea or coffee with a cup of sugar.

I finished school at the age of sixteen and began full time work at our farm. I was now old enough and strong enough to work as a man. Circumstances were such that I could not continue with any further studies for the time being as the next in line to inherit my work was not yet old enough to take over. This pause in my education gave me the opportunity to join the rural fire brigade in our village and to learn and experience more in my life.

During this time I met a nice young girl. Her name was Alexandra and she lived in a neighbouring village that was about 3 kms away. We could only see each other at weekends, mainly on Sunday afternoons providing that I had no farm duties. She became extremely fond of me and this concerned me greatly. I had plans for my future and these plans did not include settling down. I wanted to continue my education by going on to agricultural college as soon as I could. The situation eventually became even more awkward for both of us as I found that I could not fully reciprocate her feelings for me.

My parents were pleased that I wanted to continue my studies and were only too pleased to assist me. When my younger brother, Geniek, finished school and could take over my duties and responsibilities on the farm, my opportunity arose. In 1935, at the age of nineteen, I enrolled in the agricultural college in Mientnem. This was a suburb of Garwolin, a large town around 25 kms from Zwola. My enrollment was accepted and to my great delight I was fortunate enough to be awarded a scholarship. This helped to reduce my parents' commitment in supporting me while I was at the college. I loved college life and the routines involved in living and studying at such an establishment. All students lived at the college and were expected to work as well as study. We were all assigned duties and chores that had to be done before studies began and after the studies finished each day.  The college was largely self-supporting which meant we grew our own fruit and vegetables as well as raised sheep and cattle to provide meat for the college menu. In this way we were able to practice what we were studying. Our days were full and it was only on weekends, after duties and chores were finished, that we could get out and go into town for a short time.

During my time in college I was not able to return to Zwola very often. Although Mientnem was only 25 kms from Zwola it might as well have been much more. There was no public transport between the towns so you had to walk the 50 km round trip. If you were lucky enough, you might find someone with a horse and cart that was heading in your direction to save some of the walk. This enforced separation and my very infrequent returns to Zwola had the effect of dampening my relationship with Alexandra. I was fully engrossed in my new scholastic life and Alexandra's life was developing without me. Eventually she became just a pleasant memory.

3

Further Studies

In 1936, at the age of 21, I finished my studies at the agricultural college. Now, after 18 months of schooling, it was time for us to put into practice what we had learned. The college arranged for its students to obtain work experience by working on selected farms throughout the country. The farm selected for me was near a town called Helm Lubelski, 200 kms from Mientne. My life changed inexplicably when I went to Mientne. In just a couple of years I had left home to start college life and now I was going so much further away, further than I had ever been before. Also, for the first time in my life I was to be paid for my work as well. My wage was to be the princely sum of 20 Zlotys per month.

It took almost 15 hours of traveling by train, bus and then on foot to reach my destination. Fortunately, the college arranged and paid for the travel. I only had a small amount of money that was sent by my parents and that would not have been sufficient to cover my fares and provide some "living money" until I received my first pay. The farm to which I was assigned was about 15 hectares in size and was used primarily for dairy farming. However, they also grew some crops and raised pigs. Like all farms it also had a large garden for growing fruit and vegetables, largely for home consumption. The farm was run by a farmer, his wife and their three children. The eldest child, a young woman, was studying textiles at college and living away from home. She only returned for holidays and the odd weekend. I was made very welcome and treated as one of the family for the time I stayed with them.

My duties and responsibilities were to help the farmer to increase his yield in milk and cream, crops and pork. On the dairy side, I prepared various feed mixtures for the cows, measured their milk output and then tested the milk for fat content. For cropping, I conducted soil tests, applied fertilizers and co-operated with the farmer on the type of crops to be planted. I was also responsible for the rearing of the pigs and their eventual delivery to the abattoir.

Meticulous records were always kept of what was done, the cost and the results. These records enabled me to evaluate the results of my endeavours and to ensure that budgets were met.

During November of that year, I received a letter informing me that I was required to undergo medical and physical tests for the purposes of military service. All young men, on reaching twenty-one years of age, were required to undergo such tests for induction into compulsory military service. My tests were to be held in a town near Zwola but as I was some 200 kms away I applied for, and was granted, permission to have the tests in a town near the farm. The test regime was of very high standards as the military could be selective from the number of potential recruits. I was not surprised when I passed all of the tests. My lifestyle and work responsibilities ensured that I was fit and healthy as well as physically strong and supple. My fitness and health are attributes that I continue to have to this day. As I was still studying at the time, my induction into national service was deferred. The night following my tests I dreamt that I was a soldier, fighting a war against the Germans. In this dream I managed to survive a bayonet charge. I did not know then that this dream was a premonition of something that was to happen just a few years later.

Once my year of work experience was completed I was assigned to a course of further study at an Advanced Agricultural College. The college was in a village called Krasny-Staw. This study would take a further six months and was designed to round off and complete my education, particularly in the subjects of veterinary science and animal husbandry. I was to live-in again and once more had to rely on my parents for financial assistance. For six months I would no longer have an earning capacity.

Those six months passed very quickly and once I graduated I was offered a position as an Agricultural Instructor. This was actually a public service position in a little country town called Naleczof. My role was to liaise with the local farmers, to teach them farming methods, and to offer advice when necessary. My overall goal was to assist them in improving their farming methods to increase their yields of milk and crops.

I was now able to earn my own living for the first time without being reliant in some way on my parents. They had always stood by me and provided whatever assistance they could afford. I will always be grateful to them for everything they did. For my work I was to be paid 60 Zlotys per month. This would increase to 80 Zlotys if my work was deemed to be satisfactory after a three month probationary period. With me off their hands financially, my parents were now better placed to support other members of the family with their educations.

I found myself some comfortable board and lodgings for 20 Zlotys per month and settled down to my new work. There was another instructor working with me so we were able to divide up our region to best suit ourselves. Our work required us to visit each of the farms in our designated area and provide assistance with their ongoing problems and difficulties. At the same time, we could make them aware of advances in agriculture and animal husbandry. We could also assist with veterinary problems they might be experiencing as we had some training in this regard. Some of these visits to the farms would need overnight stays, particularly when it was necessary to conduct milk tests. I was always made to feel welcome by the farmers and their families. I loved the work and developed a strong bond with the people and the community in which I was working.

After only eight months in my position, my life took another turn. I received a letter to report to Radom 72 Infantry Regiment to begin my eighteen months of military service. My deferment was now over and a new chapter of my life was about to begin.

4

Military Life

In the 1930s it was regarded as an honour to be conscripted for military service. Indeed, it was expected by the community that every fit young man would do his duty. Those who did were afforded considerable respect and honour. From the large pool of potential recruits, the military selected only the fittest and smartest and I was one of them.

I reported to the camp as ordered. At the same time I felt some trepidation and excitement at the prospect of life in the military. For those who have never experienced any form of regimented life, it can come as a bit of a shock. Once you walk through the doors you must almost immediately conform to military rules and regulations. You are subjected to a life controlled by military Officers and Non-Commissioned Officers (NCOs). It can be intimidating and in some cases frightening. All this was waiting for me, a young man who until recently had never been far from home and still quite naïve in many ways of the world. Fortunately, I am a fast learner so I was able to quickly adapt to my new life and then go with the flow.

Our accommodation was in large barracks buildings, large enough to house a whole company of soldiers (which was approximately 100 men). Within the barracks there was a separate room for our commander while the NCOs and recruits were assigned to the double bunks throughout the barracks. Overall, our accommodation was quite comfortable, even though it was a little cramped. We shared a large external kitchen and dining area with the other companies in our battalion. The meals were prepared by military cooks and the quality was both satisfactory and sufficient for our needs. My only real complaint was that the coffee being served was pre-sweetened but insufficient for my taste buds, and there were no other supplies of sugar to supplement the taste.

There was also a large separate ablutions block that provided hand basins, showers and toilets. This facility was shared with all the other companies so each company was placed on a timed roster for mornings and evenings to ensure everyone had a fair opportunity to use the amenities.

Basic training was a physical grind. We rose early each morning to a daily routine of physical exercises, marching drills, weapon drills and shooting at the rifle range. At the end of the day we went to bed exhausted. When not involved in something physical there were lectures, barracks inspections, cleaning of boots, military equipment and paraphernalia, and cleaning of weapons, to name but a few of our tasks. Generally, there was little time to be wasted. The Officers and NCOs could always find something to occupy any spare time available.

Once basic training finished, our lives changed again. The strict discipline eased and each person had more time for themselves and was free to follow their own pursuits and pastimes when not required for duty.

Everyone still rose early but the day was not as hectic as in basic training. This did not mean that training and drills slackened or stopped, but that it was all done in a more humane manner.

During our basic training, each recruit was required to undergo an IQ aptitude test. Whoever organised and conducted the tests must have liked my results because a short time after basic training ended (I was now a Private rather than a Recruit) I was selected to attend an Under-Officer (Non Commissioned Officer's) course. This course was over a period of six months and provided special training. On completion of the course I was promoted to Lance Corporal. Two months later I was again promoted, this time to a full Corporal.

For some time we were hearing whispers that all was not well in Europe and that there was a possibility that war was coming. These whispers became very loud as the government of Poland was openly arranging new alliances and mutual defence pacts with neighbouring countries and shoring up its existing alliances and pacts. Historically, Poland's geographic location within Europe meant that it was a gateway to the countries in the north, east or south. Anyone with designs on the conquest of Europe had to first take control of this gateway.

Our fears were dramatically confirmed when it was announced that Germany and the Russian communists had come to an agreement on a mutual non-aggression pact. This pact had been arranged between their foreign ministers, Ribbentrop and Molotov. In one swoop the Germans had removed any fears they may have had about Russian resistance to their plans and at the same time turned them into their allies. For a number of years the Russians were actively expanding their own communist empire by taking control of countries such as Belarus and the Ukraine. This new pact now removed some previous potential obstacles to reaching their own expansion objectives. Further, the pact immediately heightened the tensions and fears of other countries like Poland because there were now two potentially "vicious tigers ready to pounce on some defenseless sheep".

The state of affairs that now dominated Europe had a major impact on the Polish armed forces. Military service was immediately expanded to increase the number of trained men under arms and the military reserves were being rearmed and made ready. For myself and the other soldiers, our training intensified and there was a new and real mix of excitement and fear in the air. There was now a real and genuine fear amongst the civilian population, who now feared the worst.

Hitler and his Nazis were making demands with menaces on Poland, as indeed they were also doing to many other European nations. The prospect of war affected me just like anyone else. I did not want war but I was a citizen of Poland and, as I saw it, it was my duty to fight if that became necessary. I had confidence that our military could hold its own but then I did not know or begin to comprehend what the Germans and Russians were capable of unleashing against us.

5

War Erupts

In July 1939, I received orders that I was being immediately transferred to the south of Poland. I was to join to a newly formed regiment called the 2nd Pulk Karpaty (Second Regiment Karpaty).

After travelling approximately 400 kms over a day and a night, firstly by train and then by military convoy, I arrived in a small town named Dukla. From there I was taken to a village called Jasliska where my new battalion was stationed. Jasliska is 15 kms from Dukla and only about 5 kms from the Czechoslovakian border. Intelligence sources felt that if the Germans were to invade Poland through Czechoslovakia, this would be the most likely sector for their advance. Perhaps the fact that the Germans were massing troops along that border was a little bit of a give-away to the ordinary soldier like myself.

On arrival, I was introduced to the Commanding Officer of the battalion, ranked Captain. I was then taken to meet the section of twenty soldiers who were now under my command. We all understood that there was probably little time. I had to get to know each of them quickly, as they had to get to know me. Like any group, we had to develop a mutual trust and confidence in each other before we were tested in battle.

We were informed that the Germans were now poised to attack. They had the luxury of deciding the time and place and all we could do was wait and hope that we were in the best position when they did. If we were to survive the initial onslaught it was imperative that our trenches and fortifications were in good order. We received orders to dig deep, and then more orders followed to dig deeper. It became obvious to everyone that this was no drill and we were in for the real thing.

As it turned out, while we waited, the Germans invaded across the Czech border about 20 kms away from my battalion's defensive positions. The date was the 1st of September 1939 and I was not quite twenty-four years of age. The war had now begun and up to this time I had not even seriously considered whether I might survive or die or even be seriously wounded. Most soldiers are optimists, believing that bad things will always happen to someone else and never to themselves.

The first day of the war began with a beautiful morning. It was far too pleasant to have to witness the horrors and deaths of so many in just that morning alone. The news now reached us confirming that the Germans had invaded and that we were now actually at war. I am not sure how I felt about the news because it was something that we were all expecting and it was only a matter of when. Just after the news had time to sink in, my battalion received orders to immediately pack up and pull back to Dukla and begin preparations to defend the town. The Germans had broken through our defensive lines in another sector of the border and were now quickly advancing in the direction of Dukla. There was also concern that if my battalion stayed at its present location, it might be cut off and encircled by the advancing German forces.

To compound our misery we were also informed that the Russians had invaded from the east. We suspected that it was highly likely that the Communists would eventually invade as well. Once the German offensive began, it did not take long before the Communists also crossed the border and occupied part of Poland. There is no doubt in my mind that this was done with Hitler's prior approval. Stalin tried to justify the actions of the communist forces by saying that they were only reclaiming territory that had belonged to Russia at one time. Poland suddenly found herself between the steel anvil of the Germans and the big hammer and sickle of the Russians and was now fighting for survival on two fronts. The "vicious tigers" had pounced.

We commenced the pull back to Dukla as soon as practicable. This was a forced march and we quickly reached the town arriving at about 10 am. Dukla was a small, tidy and quite picturesque town. Unfortunately, it was largely destroyed in the following German bombardments. The town was located amongst low rolling hills that were covered in part by forested areas and rolling pastures. Farmhouses were located throughout the area, particularly near the road that led to Dukla and beyond. Most houses were vacant, with the inhabitants having left the area fearing that the war was about to begin.

The battalion approached the outskirts of town, still some five hundred or so metres from the town centre. Unknown to us was the fact that the first German advance of troops had beaten us there. Their advance units had created a defensive line along the top of a small hill that overlooked the road on which we were marching. My section's task was to act as scouts and we were positioned on the battalion's flank, a little distance from the main body of troops. My scouting party advanced through the space between the road and the German positions. We were not aware that some of the leading Germans were already here and waiting on the hill above us.

Suddenly, all hell broke loose. The Germans opened fire and everyone scattered. The grumbles and aches and pains of the forced march were instantly forgotten with everyone being desperate to get behind some sort of cover. Fortunately for the troops on the road, the road was actually dug into the side of the hill and the embankment was facing the German positions. This embankment and the ditches beside the road provided natural defensive trenches and were used by most of our battalion for cover. It also provided a good redoubt over which we could return fire up the hill.

My scouting party was in an open field just above the road when a machine gun opened fire from a range of about 400 metres. We were the closest group of soldiers to the German positions, so we attracted most of their initial attention and fire. We dived to the ground, each of us trying to make ourselves as small a target as possible. I learned that it is very difficult to hit a prone lying target from such a long distance, even with a machine gun. As for myself, some bullets missed me by what seemed like inches but one bullet actually touched and ricocheted off my helmet. Fortunately, it caused me no harm or injury. My luck was certainly in on that day.

Most of my men, particularly the ones nearer the road, had been able to scurry and crawl back to the road and its cover. However, I and some of my men found ourselves to be in a very precarious position. There was no substantial cover or protection in our immediate vicinity. To survive we had get out of there and find a much less exposed position. The problem facing us was how to move without attracting another stream of bullets from the machine gun above us. I had been extremely lucky once already, but did not know for how long I could expect my luck to last, particularly if I stayed where I was.

Despite the battle raging all around me, I found that I had managed to keep my wits and senses about me. As an NCO and at that time the scout for my company, I carried a set of binoculars. Using these I was able to locate and identify the German positions on the hill and pinpoint the exact location of the machine gun that kept raking our position. This was also my first sighting of real German troops, even if it was with binoculars from a range of 400 metres or so. They appeared to be dressed in dark or black uniforms (I later found it was a shade of blue) and each wore a dark coloured helmet. Throughout the day I often saw flashes of sunlight reflected from some of their helmets.

With the range finder in the binoculars I could calculate the distance of the machine gun from where I lay. This enabled me to adjust the sights on my rifle to the correct distance before taking aim and firing my first bullet "in anger". Most battles are fought over shorter distances of 100 to 200 metres so the rifle sights are usually set for this range. With such settings it is highly unlikely that anyone could hit a target over a longer range, particularly a small target. However, "Lady Luck" continued to smile upon me. The shot I fired seemed to have the effect of ceasing the firing from the machine gun. I do not know whether I had managed to hit the gunner or hit the machine gun itself, or whether the machine gun had simply jammed at that point, or perhaps they simply ran out of ammunition and couldn't reload quickly enough. Whatever the reason, the lull in the firing enabled the men still with me to crawl back into the drainage ditch beside the road and into some reasonable protection. The machine gun soon resumed its fire and maintained its fire on and off throughout the rest of the day. Somehow we had all managed to get back and survive to fight another day. "Lady Luck" had indeed smiled on me a second time that same day.

Throughout the remainder of the day the Germans troops kept peppering our makeshift defensive lines. At their disposal they had better weapons in the form of modern and sophisticated machine guns and field artillery. By comparison, our machine guns were old but serviceable and far fewer were available to us. We had no field artillery apart from one old anti-tank gun. The Germans were supported by a number of tanks (we could hear them rumbling in the background, out of sight). We were greatly outgunned, but what we lacked in firepower we made up in guts and determination. We were determined to defend our country and to show them what the soldiers of the Polish army could do.

Later that morning one of the German tanks showed itself on the front line. I can only assume that it was sent forward to give us a taste of their high-powered weaponry. We already knew that they had tanks somewhere along their lines as we had heard them the previous day rumbling past on the other side of the hill and in the woods. Fortunately, some time had passed since the initial contact with the Germans and our gunners had had sufficient time to set up the anti-tank gun. The appearance of the tank on the hill was the chance they were waiting for and they quickly engaged it. Their first shell hit and destroyed the tank. It was a wonderful sight and a boost to our morale to see the tank erupt into a cloud of smoke and then explode into flames. I don't know what this did to German morale but it was the only tank we saw for the rest of the day. It remained in plain sight as a smoking reminder to the Germans that we meant business.

Despite the German overall superiority in manpower (it was suggested later that we were actually outnumbered in the realm of about 10 to 1) and their superior weaponry, we managed to hold our haphazard defensive line. We had miraculously suffered no major casualties in the day's exchanges of fire and I would think that the German casualties were also relatively light as well. I do not know what casualties the German tank crew may have received.

Perhaps the Germans were just not ready for us at the time we arrived at Dukla and began firing as a matter of course. The range was great, so it would have been difficult to effectively hit targets. By firing they were only giving their positions away. Alternatively, they may have just tried to pin us down to stop us from moving into the town itself and using it as a defensive position. They would have realised that there was little or no chance of assaulting us before the rest of their troops had arrived and got into position.

After the initial onslaught there were occasional breaks in the firing. These breaks provided us with some respite and enabled the battalion to re-deploy the companies into better defensive positions and even to construct some minor fortifications. During one of the breaks, the battalion cooks were able to distribute a hot meal that they had prepared. The field kitchen was some distance away in Dukla and had not been subjected to any attacks up to then. The cooks took the opportunity to put together some hot food. This hot food proved to be a great boost to us all.

Few of our soldiers had ever been under fire before that day. Now they had fought their first action and then a number of subsequent actions, all during the previous few hours. It is very hard to describe how being involved in your first hostile action really feels. The experience affects everyone differently, varying from total calmness in some people to panic or sheer terror in others. For others it is something in between. Most veterans, when asked how they felt the first time would most likely answer that you wouldn't understand unless you experienced it yourself. Irrespective of your initial reaction to being shot at, your training takes over and you begin to react in the way you have been trained. What is universal however is that everyone feels extremely tired, hungry and thirsty once it is over, and the euphoria of realising that they have survived gradually subsides. The meal we received was for me heaven sent. It takes something like this to bring you back to earth and change your focus. Unbeknown to any of us at that time, it was to be almost the last worthwhile meal that we would have for the next ten days or so.

Towards dusk there was a further lull in the firing, but as dusk was falling the Germans mounted their major attack and came at us with force. They came with bayonets fixed and with the intention to break through our lines before total darkness had set in. During the afternoon, and unbeknowns to us, the Germans had managed to move some troops into the woods and some into the deserted farmhouses near our lines. Now they were coming to destroy the resistance that would enable them to resume their drive into the heart of Poland. When they arrived we met them in a desperate man-to-man and hand-to-hand combat.

It started with just a few shots and our men calling to each other that it seemed that the Germans were coming. Suddenly, shapes appeared before us in the fading light. The tempo of the firing increased rapidly as they approached our lines. The noise of battle is impossible to accurately describe. There was the mix of yelling and screaming amongst the noise of weapons being fired all at once. It was at this time that I was the target of a bayonet charge by one of the Germans. This soldier had managed to make his way around the back of a farmhouse in the twilight and then sneak up from our flank. Suddenly, he just appeared before me and lunged forward with his rifle and bayonet. Somehow, I was able to parry his thrust and his bayonet hit my rifle and was deflected away from my body. His loss of momentum enabled me to knock him down with a blow to his head with my rifle butt. In a do or die contest such as this there are no rules except to do whatever you must to protect your own life. His actual attack lasted only a fraction of a second. I managed to club him and my blow disabled and took the fight right out of him. The brutal contest was over in just a few seconds. I am grateful that he tried to bayonet me rather than shoot me first. Perhaps he had a rush of blood and subconsciously decided that he was going to bayonet a Pole. Whatever his reasoning, I have no doubt that he would have killed me had circumstances not gone my way. In my mind I can still picture this soldier trying to crawl away from me so that I would not kill him. I let him go. He was beaten and had had enough. Perhaps he also managed to survive the war and every now and then remembers how his life nearly ended at the hands of a Polish soldier on the first day of the war.

Some time later, after all the fighting had subsided, I found that his bayonet had actually inflicted a wound. His bayonet had sliced open my thumb, probably when it was deflected off my rifle. In the heat of the battle I had not felt the stab nor any pain. I did not notice the bleeding and it wasn't until later, once I cooled down, that I realised I had been wounded. I managed to bandage the wound with a field dressing and that would have to suffice until I could get some proper medical attention. The pain that comes with any such injury always comes later, once the action is all over and the adrenalin coursing through your body has subsided. So it did for me, but I was too busy to worry about it then.

We had beaten the Germans back and in the process given them a mighty bloody nose. This was the only frontal assault that they would attempt. They began pulling back, at the same time taking many of their wounded and the bodies of the dead with them. The shooting and noise began to abate and in the darkness all that was left was the destruction caused by warfare. Worn out men who had survived the onslaught, the screams and moans of the wounded and the bodies of the dead.

I do not know how many casualties we sustained that night but I would think that the Germans suffered more. Sadly, one of the men in my section was killed in the hand-to-hand fighting. The other nineteen had survived and each had their own story of survival to tell. Unfortunately, many other men - some I knew and others who were just comrades-in-arms - were now dead or wounded. Eventually, the medics and stretcher- bearers came and did whatever they could to patch up the wounded before evacuating them into the town. I would not see any of the wounded again. The bodies of the dead, Poles and Germans, were eventually removed and taken away for burial.

Once everything had settled down I remembered the dream that I had had on the night of my national service medical. This reality of the bayonet attack was so very similar to what I could remember of that dream. The scar on my thumb is now my reminder of how close I came to being killed or badly wounded, and that I had been so extremely fortunate three times in that twenty-four hour period. I suppose that, just like the German soldier, it wasn't my time.

Their attacks against our lines changed to probing, patrol skirmishes and sniping. This pattern continued throughout the night and into the next morning. Perhaps the Germans needed a break to lick their wounds just as we did. During the night the Germans began shelling over our defensive lines and into the town of Dukla itself. The subsequent destruction of the township of Dukla was due to their continuous artillery barrages. Some of these shells hit a building that we were using as an arsenal and as a depot for our personal kit and possessions. Amongst these possessions was my suitcase that contained all my important agricultural notes and photos. Before the war I had bought a new suit and that was in my suitcase as well. My eighteen months of military service was due to end on 15th September (a fortnight after the outbreak of the war) and I had bought the suit with the intention of wearing it on my discharge back into civilian life. The war changed all that and my discharge came many years later with my demobilisation after the war ended. The field kitchen that provided us with that marvelous meal the previous day had all its provisions stored in that building as well. Most of the town, including our depot building, burned all night and almost everything was destroyed.

Early next morning, on September 2nd, we learned that the Germans had managed to break through another battalion further down our defensive lines and were now pouring through the breech they had created. Their breakout was again about to threaten our position from the rear. To add to our woes they had also managed to damage our communication networks. This made it almost impossible for any units to contact their command centres or any of their neighbouring units without using runners. The loss of our ability for Central Command to quickly issue orders or provide up-to-date information put our forces in the area into untenable positions. Eventually, our Officer-in-Charge, Captain Kazmierczak, issued orders for our battalion to retreat.

Now that the Germans had achieved their breakthrough, the fighting in our immediate sector died down. Our last night in Dukla was relatively quiet.

6

Retreat

There was much sadness and disappointment when the orders for our retreat came through. Overnight we had proven ourselves to be a match for the Germans. We had fought courageously and the Germans could not break through our lines nor break our spirit. Yet, the adverse positions in other sectors along the border forced the decision that we now had to pull back from the invaders. In hindsight, the order to retreat may have been in all our best interests. We were now running short of ammunition and all of the other supplies and provisions that we would need to keep functioning as an effective fighting force. The depot fire did not exactly cripple our fighting abilities, but it would make life very difficult from now on. With what was going on all over Poland at that time, there was no possibility of our battalion being reinforced or resupplied.

We were ordered to withdraw to the south towards the Hungarian border, and were confident that once we arrived there we would be made welcome and receive assistance in supplies and equipment, and that our wounded would receive the care they desperately needed.

The most direct and possibly the safest route for our units to retreat was through the mountains. There were many roads and tracks that could be followed, and if care was taken there was a good chance of getting through undetected and relatively unscathed. Each battalion was to make its own way to a designated position on the border. This strategy was adopted to avoid any build up or large concentrations of troops retreating along the same route. For security reasons we were not given any indication as to our destination at the border.

We pulled back from our defensive lines and commenced the first stage of our retreat. It was early in the morning of 2nd September and it was difficult to believe that we had been at war for one day already. The morning was again fine and warm, pleasant weather in which to begin our march. It may have been an omen as well as a blessing because the weather remained fine and warm for the duration of the retreat. The easiest way to describe a retreat is that it is really one forced march after another. We marched both day and night, resting and sleeping when and wherever we could.

Our only possessions were the clothes we wore, our basic equipment, our rifles and the little ammunition we each carried. Everything else was lost in the fire. We had no food and so from then on would have to rely on anything that we would be given and anything else that we could pilfer and scavenge. Every now and then some patriotic and generous farmers or inhabitants of small villages would give us some food as we passed through. It was mainly bread and milk, but when you are so hungry such simple fare tastes like manna from heaven. They helped as much as they could but once the food was shared around there wasn't that much for each individual. The only other source of food available was fruit and raw vegetables. There were many orchards in the farms beside the roads. It was late summer so there was still some fruit on the trees. The orchards we came across were raided mercilessly. Deserted farms still had some vegetable in the gardens and the barns and outhouses could hold stores of corn or potatoes. Water was not a problem because we could readily refill our water bottles at every creek, dam or pond we passed by.

Military etiquette also went out the window. We now had nothing with which to shave or to clean our equipment, weapons or boots. We had lost nearly everything. By the end of the withdrawal we would all be wearing some long stubble, our clothing would be tatty and ragged and we would all smell after not having the opportunity to bathe. Within a relatively short time I managed to grow a luxurious beard that I kept for some time afterwards. We had no change of clothes, nor were we able to wash anything, particularly our underwear, as we never stopped long enough for any washing to dry. The problems of a lack of military etiquette were really minor compared to other challenges we would have to face during our journey.

Fatigue, hunger and misery became the constant companions of each soldier. Continuous marching with little rest or sleep and lack of food soon turned each of us into walking robots. We had mastered the art of marching for long periods while blocking out the sensations of fatigue, aching feet and muscles and the stomach pains from constant hunger. The mind is incredible in what it can do. We could march and yet be in a sort of sleep where the brain goes into a sort of idle mode. At the slightest hint of danger, the mind instantly rouses and refocuses. This is not something that soldiers can be taught but is something they develop as a form of self-preservation. Although the days were fine and warm, nights were a different matter. Most nights were becoming quite cool so whenever we halted for a rest, we looked for some sheltered position where we could put our heads down. To be able to have the use of a barn, particularly if there was some straw or anything else that could be used to create a makeshift bed to sleep in, was a luxury.

To compound our problems, we had to come to terms with a new enemy. This enemy did not wear a uniform or carry a gun but was potentially just as deadly. Over the centuries when Poland's borders waxed and waned, people from many different nationalities settled there. Some still had strong allegiances with their Germanic past or to other countries. For example, there were large numbers of Ukrainian expatriates living in parts of Poland, having fled from Russian domination of their homelands. Large numbers of these expats were now wittingly or unwittingly collaborating with the Germans. Some groups of people wanted Poland to fall under German control, while other groups believed in the promises that Hitler made for his vision of a better Europe under the Nazis.

These collaborators were observing our every movement. It is impossible for anyone to tell whether a person standing by the side of the road, looking out their window or offering some food, may have the ulterior motive of gathering intelligence. It was not unusual to be asked our names and our unit as we trudged up the road. We had been warned that all manner of information was being gathered and passed to the Germans through their sleeper agents. The Germans had been planning their invasion for some time in advance. To put some plans into effect they sought out and recruited these expats and other sympathisers to set up information gathering and spy networks. There was very little that we could do to stop these collaborators, except to be guarded in what we said.

There were other dangers facing us as well. As a personal warning, we had been told that some Ukrainians had previously assaulted individual soldiers, those who had become detached from their unit or lagged behind. A group of men would grab the soldier's weapon and set upon him giving him a severe beating. In some cases the soldiers had died from the beatings. I think that I was almost a victim of one of these assaults when I developed a nose bleed as we were passing through a village. As we approached a puddle by the side of the road I decided to stop and wash my face. I yelled out to my commanding officer that I was stopping but he and the rest of the men kept going on. Suddenly, I found myself to be alone and I noticed that two men, one from each side, began approaching me. Fortunately, there are many similarities between the Polish and Ukrainian languages so that when they spoke to each other I managed to understand their intentions. I raised my rifle and yelled for them to back off or I would shoot. They grudgingly did so as they could see that I was prepared to follow through with my threat. I then moved off quickly and caught up with my unit.

It was not known by the ordinary fighting soldiers,

but the mutual defence alliance was proving too much for the Rumanians. The value of their commitment to their mutual defence pact had become questionable. At some time after the war had begun the Rumanians had decided that it was no longer in their own best interests to become militarily involved as allies of Poland. In fact, as the war continued it eventually became evident that their government had begun to actively support and collaborate with the Nazis. Poland was finding herself to be increasingly isolated and responsible for her own defence.

France and Great Britain declared war on Germany once the invasion of Poland began. They could only offer us words of support and make demands on the Germans - demands that were not taken very seriously. Neither France nor Britain were prepared for a war. Britain in particular had accepted Hitler's earlier assurances of non-aggression and therefore made no real effort to improve her preparedness. Before either country could come to a war footing they needed to mobilise their armed forces and turn their industries to the production of munitions and equipment with which to fight a war. This would take some time and time was something that Poland was quickly running out of.

At the time of their war declarations, Britain and France had little to offer Poland apart from some garrison troops in Europe. These troops fought the Germans in Holland and Belgium. The battles were rather one- sided and resulted in the British being eventually driven back and then evacuating most of their troops back to Britain from the port of Dunkirk. Once the British left and France recalled its remaining troops, the whole of Europe, the Middle East and North

Africa fell into the hands of the "vicious tigers" and the new Italian fascist, Mussolini.

A few months later, the French Government readily capitulated. The German invasion and their triumphant entrance into the city of Paris took less time than it took for Poland to fall. Britain and her empire then found themselves to be virtually alone against the might of the German war machine together with its collaborators and allies.

On the fifth day of our retreat, it was decided that our battalion should have an extended rest. The pace of our retreat was slowing and was further delayed by our wounded and the men who were simply just worn out. The rest was indeed welcomed, as we had been on the road for five days and nights with only short breaks. Everyone was reaching the end of their tether, in a constant state of fatigue and suffering from the torment of constant hunger.

The site for our camp was to be a farm which had a number of large outbuildings. We saw this as an opportunity to take advantage of the cover these buildings would provide. It was intended that we should have our first decent rest under some modest shelter. The farm was still inhabited, so the farmer and his family would stay in the farmhouse and we would use the outbuildings. For the last five days we had had to lie or sit beside the road or in the fields or under a tree in the forest. On this night, however, we settled down in the luxury of shelter in a barn.

Some time around midnight, our sentries spotted a German patrol approaching the farm. They waited to see what the patrol was doing in case they were just passing by, but in the end had no option but to open fire. This action forced the Germans to quickly move away and disappear into the night. There was no indication whether there were any German casualties. We prepared ourselves for a possible attack just in case the patrol was a scouting party for a much larger force. Fortunately, nothing eventuated after the contact with the sentries. I can only guess as to the reason why their patrol made its way to our position. Perhaps our presence was earlier reported to the Germans and the patrol came out to find our exact location and probe our strength. Alternatively they may have been looking for somewhere to bunk down for the night themselves and picked the spot we were already occupying. Whatever the reason, unless they were actually looking for us, they must have received a rude shock.

Now that we had been located, the patrol would have certainly reported the contact. Our prudent reaction was to leave the area as soon as possible. Everyone was now awake and, as we had nothing to pack, we were ready to move almost immediately. The action used up more of our already depleted ammunition supply. We were now down to only a couple of bullets for each man and they would not last long if we came upon more than just a patrol. We received orders to continue our march as soon as possible. It was necessary for us to keep away from the main roads and to only use the country or secondary roads. Our battalion had been located, whether they were looking for us or not, and if we were to reach our border destination we had to adopt a less overt avenue of retreat.

Early one afternoon, on either the seventh or eighth day, as we approached an area that was only lightly wooded, we could hear the sounds of a light aeroplane flying somewhere above us. We immediately roused from our robotic state and continued forward rather cautiously. Evidently, the pilot had seen us or possibly seen some movement below him, because he began circling. With each pass he descended slightly. The plane did not have the dreaded German swastika under its wings but had colours similar to the roundels under the wings of English planes. Our anxiety eased somewhat as the plane seemed to be from friendly forces. After several low passes, the pilot must have been satisfied with what he had seen or lost interest because he then flew off. All that was left was the sounds of the receding aeroplane and soldiers staring up into the sky.

We resumed our march and I am sure that everyone was now quite alert to the dangers that could very quickly arise. Each additional day and night of marching brought us closer to the Hungarian border. We had had only one contact with the Germans before now, the contact with the patrol and now the aeroplane that may have been a false alarm. Surely the Germans had some idea where we and other Polish units might be. The collaborators must surely have identified us and pinpointed our positions and direction of travel over the last week.

As we progressed further into the sparsely wooded area, sounds of more aeroplanes could be heard. The planes were heading in our direction. We were instantly on guard but as they approached, flying quite low, we saw that they had the same markings as the plane we had seen earlier. Perhaps the earlier plane was returning and bringing some of his mates with him. As they flew nearer, many of the men left their cover and stood to cheer and wave. In the short time it took for the planes to descend further towards us, it became obvious that they had not come to waggle their wings, they had come to drop bombs. Sheer terror, and in some cases blind panic, set in once it was realised that we had been so foolish.

The planes were so low that it seemed as if their bombs were detonating as soon as they were released. The first bombs struck before many men could dive for good cover. Fortunately, the planes were not bombers or fighter-bombers and so the bombs they carried were small and very difficult to aim effectively. They dropped their bombs and circled, but they had not finished with us yet. They dived again and began strafing those men who were lying on the ground and those running to get behind some sort of cover. The only real cover available was under and behind trees. It did not help that the area was only lightly covered with trees and some trees were small enough to provide little or no protection. I managed to dive under the canopy of a large oak tree, one of the few larger trees in my immediate vicinity.

Soldiers sometimes get the feeling that the enemy is concentrating solely on killing them and is applying all its resources and energies to that one objective. After making several strafing runs, two of the planes flew off leaving one that was circling and looking for more targets. I felt that the pilot of this plane was out to get me when bullets from his machine guns struck the tree trunk on at least two occasions. Every time he circled I would move around the tree trunk keeping it between me and him. After several more passes he must have decided that he was not going to get me this time and so flew off.

An eerie silence descended on the woods as we lay there trying to make sense of all that had happened. It was a miracle that only one soldier was wounded and there were no deaths from the attack. The wounded soldier was evacuated by a local farmer, carried on his horse and cart to a hospital in a nearby town. The bombing and strafing took a heavy mental toll on many of the men.

A short time passed as we licked our wounds and allowed the ringing in our ears to subside, and then the march recommenced. We were now a lot smarter and wiser in the way we conducted ourselves. Being bombed and strafed was another first for us, and we had to learn our lessons very quickly if most of us were to survive. We would never come out of cover to cheer and wave for any aeroplane again, no matter what the markings appeared to be. We now also understood that the closer we got to the border, the greater the danger was likely to be. The grind of the march continued and we continued to be constantly tired, sore and hungry.

On the tenth day of our retreat, we arrived at a small town called Kolo. We were now only 20kms or so from the Hungarian border. Perhaps this was the secret destination. Everything in the town and surrounding area was quiet. The local townspeople said that there were no German or other troops in the area. On the strength of this information, and the fact that we had not seen any German activity since the bombings, our headquarters decided that the battalion should enjoy an extended rest. It was obvious that many of the men were almost at the end of their tether and we were now so close to our goal.

One of the senior officers arranged for the purchase

of a large bullock and some potatoes from one of the farmers. The hungry and tired soldiers were to have a hearty meal and a rest before completing the march to the border. The animal and potatoes were duly delivered to our camp with much fanfare and delight. The battalion had within its ranks a number of people who were expert in animal butchery and they soon commenced their work. The prospect of finally receiving some good food in the form of beef and potatoes brought out the best in them. It didn't take long for the bullock to be killed, butchered and dressed, while the battalion's catering personnel prepared for the cooking. They had managed to find a large drum that could be used for the cooking process, but it first needed a thorough clean. This was done with minimum protest or complaint. Others peeled the potatoes and soon the meal preparation was underway. An aroma of cooking meat permeated throughout the camp and only added to our hunger. When the meal was finally served it was both delicious and welcome and there were no leftovers to be seen.

After a few hours of rest, we were ordered to continue our march to the Hungarian border. We were informed that the battalion was expecting to receive a desperately needed resupply of food and ammunition. This news, on top of the meal and rest, lifted everyone's spirits and we set off with high hopes. Eventually, during the march, the reality of our situation surfaced once again and doubts and other concerns crept into our minds. What if the Hungarians were unable to or refused to help or to become involved, particularly after we had come all this way and endured as much as we had. Had the townspeople told us the truth about enemy activity in the area? Could the Germans be waiting to intercept us somewhere before the border? We had little ammunition; and so any determined attack would certainly end in our defeat and ultimate surrender. It was with high expectations, together with such thoughts as these, that we began our final journey of 20kms.

7

Hungary

We were filled with much hope and anticipation as we neared the border. We had come such a long way and endured much more than we could ever have imagined, just to get to where we were. As we marched on, someone began singing. Others then took it up, and before long nearly everyone was singing. This made the final few kilometers pass very quickly.

As we came within sight of the border, the singing began to die. I am not sure what I expected to see, but there was nothing there. All we could see was one lone soldier at the Hungarian border crossing. He saw us and must have wondered why we were just standing there. Had he been closer, he would have seen the bewilderment in our eyes and the dismay in our faces. He began gesturing for us to approach and cross through the border checkpoint. At this time my feelings were very mixed and many thoughts raced through my mind. I asked myself whether the treaty was worthless and therefore there would be no troops or supplies. Perhaps they were just out of our sight, somewhere close by. Was everything just over the border? From the faces of my comrades-in-arms I could see that many had similar feelings and questions. We were to discover the answers to these questions shortly.

We were ordered to continue our march into Hungary. As we began crossing the border, the Hungarian guard came to attention and saluted. He remained that way until the whole battalion had passed through. Despite our feelings of extreme disappointment, we marched with our heads held high, our backs straight and our demeanor proud. Our arrival at the border did not provide the welcome that we expected, but we were still hoping that everything would turn out well for us.

We marched a few kilometers past the border post and on entering a large valley the battalion was called to a halt. It was now just after midday. Standing on the road and blocking our way forward were a number of Hungarian Senior Military Officers. We did not see any other Hungarian soldiers anywhere in our vicinity. The Hungarian Officers were waiting for us, so I presume they were receiving intelligence, probably from the Germans, that we were coming. Once we had halted, they approached our headquarters and met with our commanding officers. They met for some time before the meeting concluded. The Hungarian Officers left but, to our surprise, stopped only a short distance away and waited.

Shortly after the officers left, our headquarters issued orders that would give me, up to that time, the saddest moment of my life. We had been ordered to disarm and all our weapons and ammunition were to be thrown into the ditch beside the road. They informed us that our war was over and we were about to be interned within Hungary. Poland would need to continue her struggle against the Nazis without us. There was considerable anger at the order to disarm and most of the men were very reluctant to put down their weapons. These were our weapons and they had been used to good effect. Eventually, common sense prevailed and our weapons and equipment were cast into the ditch. I put my binoculars down but there was one item that I was determined to hold on to. I had a small compass and I reasoned that if I ever had the chance to escape, it would prove to be invaluable. I hid the compass in my leggings without telling anyone about it. This compass was to remain with me until 1942 when I had good reason to throw it away. Considering the number of times that I was searched, it is amazing that it was not found and, with all that we went through, that it was neither damaged nor destroyed.

The Hungarians had reneged on their treaty obligations and were now collaborating with the Nazis. We could now understand why the Germans were not actively harassing us in our retreat or trying to destroy us. They had already made arrangements with the Hungarians as to what was to happen once any Polish troops crossed their borders. The Hungarian Officers stood slightly apart from us to observe that the disarmament orders were being obeyed. History now records that, despite their collaboration, both Hungary and Romania were eventually treated by the Nazis as just another of their conquered and occupied countries. Their fate eventually paralleled Poland, firstly crushed in the hands of the Nazis and then trampled and bled under the occupation of the so-called liberating Russian Communist forces.

From the border, we were then taken to the internment camp by a train that was waiting at a station nearby. Once the disarm order had been carried out, the Hungarian Officers led our column to the station and we boarded the train. The train left almost as soon as our embarkation had been completed. We traveled for hours before reaching our destination at about 6 pm. The trip itself was unremarkable. The train travelled through areas of forest and expanses of open fields, with small towns or villages located beside the tracks every now and then. This would have been just like traveling across Poland by train. At least the carriages were reasonably comfortable for the many hours we just sat there. The trip could have been quite pleasant had not nearly everyone been suffering from feelings of betrayal, gloom and doom, mixed with the fear of what was going to happen to us now. We had not been provided with any food and water for the final march or the train trip but that was something that we were now used to.

The internment camp that was set up for us was on a large farm near the town of Sabota. This farm location meant that we were being taken across Hungary to somewhere near the Czechoslovakian border. This took us a long distance away from the Polish border. Once we had disembarked at the station, a troop of Hungarian soldiers escorted us to the camp.

Our camp was a farm comprising of a large main farmhouse, some very large barns and sheds and a number of outhouses. One of the sheds was to be used as our kitchen. The farm was actually a working concern and, as part of our right to stay there, internees who were fit enough and could work were obliged to help with the running of the farm. It was intended that the camp would become mostly self-sufficient.

Apart from our lodgings we would receive three meals a day, provided that we met the work commitment. The battalion's commissioned officers were assigned accommodation in the main farmhouse, while all other ranks had to make do with the barns and sheds. My shared accommodation was in a barn and this proved to be adequate for the time I was to stay at the camp.

It was dark by the time everything had been sorted out so most of the men laid down, made themselves as comfortable as they could and went to sleep. The next morning, after a quick wash, we were provided with breakfast. This was something that we were no longer used to. The battalion cooks had been provided with rations and they had been up since the crack of dawn and were able to provide a meal for the whole camp. This was our first meal since the feast of meat and potatoes.

After breakfast the battalion was paraded and we were addressed by our Commanding Officer. He informed us that the nation of Poland had now surrendered to the Germans. As a result, Poland's armed forces had also surrendered. Whilst we remained in Hungary we would no longer be soldiers but civilians. As civilians we were no longer under internment, but under agreement with the Hungarian authorities we could remain at the camp as non-combatants for as long as the camp remained open. Those who chose to remain were not forced to work but could volunteer to work on the camp farm or the surrounding farms. Alternatively, we could leave the camp and try and make our way back to our homes in occupied Poland or travel anywhere else in Europe that would allow us to enter. We were then informed of the camp rules and regulations under which we had to abide for the time we remained.

It is difficult to describe the feelings and anxieties that we experienced at this announcement. Over the period of the previous two weeks we had been involved in the outbreak of a world war, been attacked and fought for our lives and the survival of our country, marched hundreds of kilometers, survived the rigors of lack of food and sleep, endured constant tiredness and been bombed and strafed. Then, within the last twenty-four hours, we had been turned from a force of hardened fighting men into a large group of interned non-combatant soldiers, and then into civilians. To compound the situation, we were a long way from our own country. Poland, her people and the men and women who had fought and were still fighting for her survival had been cruelly betrayed.

Later that afternoon we were issued with new underwear and a new shirt. Everyone had been wearing the same shirts and underwear since the outbreak of the war, when our extra clothing and supplies were destroyed in the fire. We took the opportunity to have a good body wash before putting on our new clothes. What was worth keeping from our old clothes was put aside to be washed and the rest were discarded. Some of the men decided to try and shave. No-one had their own shaving gear but some were able to borrow the equipment from the battalion barber and have their first shave for a number of weeks. I decided to let my new beard grow as I had never grown a beard before and it was a bit of a novelty.

It became clear that the preference of most of the men was to return home to Poland. The war was over for us but there was still family trying to survive and most of the men saw it as their duty to return. Some actually started on their return journey as early as the following day. I had also decided to return and discussed this with two of the men with whom I had forged a bond of friendship and camaraderie since joining the battalion. We agreed to return together, but decided to stay on the farm for a few more weeks to rest and recuperate.

Life on the farm was the panacea we needed. It became easier once each of us had accepted that we weren't active soldiers any longer and that the rest of our lives were in our own hands. The pains of hunger were now gone and most of the fears, disappointments and anxieties had diminished. Each person's thinking had to change to consider what they would do now.

Generally, farmers are the same throughout Europe. They experience similar problems, and have similar grumbles - with the most common issue being the hard and continuous work. Most of us readily stepped back into lives as farmers and were appreciated for our efforts. With my background as an Agricultural Instructor I was able to assist many of the local farmers with planning and operational advice that would be of benefit to them. Having the capacity and willingness to work as hard as they did also earned many Poles a certain level of respect.

During our stay at the farm, the Red Cross distributed a card, similar to a post card, to each man. This card was to be filled out and returned to them for forwarding on to the man's family in Poland. The card would inform them that their son was alive, of his state of health and where he was located at the time of filling out the card. The completed cards were collected and dispatched by the Red Cross people to their headquarters in Geneva.

We understood that the cards would then be posted from Geneva to the home addresses. I discovered many years later that the card that I had filled out took nearly twelve months to reach my parents. This card was the first indication that they received that I was still alive. However, the card was really little consolation to them as anything could have happened to me in the year it took to reach them. In fact, at the time they received the card, I was a prisoner-of-war in a POW Stalag in Germany. There was no way that they could have been aware of that at the time the card arrived. Other parents may have rejoiced on receiving the card, unaware that their son had in fact died or been badly injured during the intervening period.

8

Into Captivity

The most direct route to Poland from where we were was north, through Czechoslovakia. The train trip to the internment camp had taken us across Hungary and we now had a large part of Czechoslovakia between the camp and Poland. The alternative was to backtrack through Hungary to the border and then to cross back somewhere near where we had originally entered.

After several weeks of rest, one of my friends and I decided that it was time to go home. The other decided to stay a little longer. We were somewhat grateful to the Hungarians for their protection and security and for providing us with the facilities in which to recover from our previous ordeals. Their government may have betrayed the Poles but their people had taken us into their midst and generally treated us well. Despite everything good about our camp and Hungary, it was not home and that is where my heart still lay.

Our return journey would have to be made on foot. The Hungarians were not about to put us on a train especially to take us back to the Polish border. There were no formal arrangements to enter or cross Czechoslovakia and we had none of the official travel or identity documents that were necessary for us to travel legitimately. Consequently, the crossing could be awkward and a little risky. We could be stopped and questioned, or possibly even arrested by the police, at any time. It was very possible that we could come across some Nazi sympathizers or collaborators in our travels and they could put our lives in jeopardy. We were prepared to accept all of these risks as there was no other means of getting home.

We left the camp one morning and made our way to the Czech border. Our only possessions were the clothes we wore and a little bag, called a bread bag. In this bag we carried some sandwiches and corn on the cob, to provide us with some food for our journey home. We had saved the sandwiches from meals at the camp and been given the corn by the farmers with whom we had worked. It was now autumn in Europe and the weather was still fine, quite warm during the day but becoming a little cool at night. We approached the border just as it was getting dark and managed to cross without any problems. There were many people crossing in both directions and the border guards did not show any real interest in us or anyone else. We were now in Czechoslovakia and unsure of what reception we would receive in our travels.

Our plan was simple. We would travel as much as possible at night and rest up during the day. This strategy would also give us the opportunity to reconnoiter the way ahead once we approached a town or village. We could also seek out any food sources such as orchards and isolated barns that we could raid at night. We were well aware that the food we carried would not sustain us for the entire journey, and so we were prepared to obtain supplies the best way we could. We were not, however, prepared to physically harm anyone in our endeavours.

The first night was fine and cool and we were easily able to see our way ahead. We kept a sharp lookout and an open ear for anyone or anything that might be coming up or down the road. To avoid being seen we would leave the road and hide behind trees and bushes until travellers had passed. As dawn broke, we had to increase our vigilance. We continued walking until the local people were rising and there was a danger that we would be seen. Being farmers ourselves, we were well aware that the Czech farmers would also be up early and moving about their farms or beginning their day's work. The sight of a couple of strangers dressed in well worn and slightly tattered military uniforms could certainly arouse their interest or suspicion. These were risks that were avoidable by hiding behind some cover.

Once the daylight strengthened, we left the road and found ourselves a good position where we could not be seen by passers-by. We had to choose a position that, while still being close to the road, provided some avenues of escape if necessary. We settled down for the day and ate some of the rations that we had brought from the camp. Then we tried to get some sleep during the day. When we awoke it was early afternoon and very little was happening outside our haven. We remained there until the evening. Once it was sufficiently dark and we were confident that we would not be easily spotted, we left our cover and set off. It was our second night travelling the roads of Czechoslovakia. We managed to cover a fair distance without any incident. Once again the night had been fine. The moonlight was sufficient for us to set a fair walking pace and there was little traffic to slow us down. After daybreak, we selected a position and left the road to bunker down for the day.

Unfortunately, our luck then ran out. As we entered the tree line beside the road, we stumbled onto an armed two man Czech military patrol. I can only guess as to the reason that this patrol was there, but I suspect that they were positioned there for the purpose of intercepting anyone like us. They could not have known that we were coming up the road, or where we would leave the road for our day's rest. However, from their position they could have intercepted us either day or night as we went past. Perhaps, if our luck held out, we could have gone into hiding before we were seen and they would not have known we were around. They may have changed their position during the day or given their position away, and we may have been able to bypass them that night. My luck could unfortunately only take me this far.

The demeanour of these soldiers towards us was not aggressive. Once we got over our initial shock, they told us not to be afraid and that they would not harm us. They claimed to be our friends and our allies against the Germans. We were two unarmed men against two men armed with rifles and pistols, and so we thought it prudent to go along with what they said and to do as we were asked. We were not in a position to argue or demand any rights. They led us to a car that was in a concealed spot not far away and one of the soldiers said that they would drive us to the Polish border. We were rather skeptical of what we had been told, however we could not see any other alternatives and so we hoped, and silently prayed, that they intended to do just as they had said.

After driving for a few hours, they turned off the road and stopped at a large solid gate in front of what appeared to be an army compound. The gate had a sign above it in large letters: "OREMOW-LAS Camp". It did not look like what you would expect to see at a Polish border post and the only guards there appeared to be Czechoslakian. The compound was located in quite a densely forested area and surrounded by a high brick fence that was topped with barbed wire. Around the perimeter there were guard towers with machine guns, manned by uniformed troops. One of the guards opened the gate and we drove through and stopped outside a large hut. I assumed that this was some sort of headquarters building and that our captors were reporting in. One of the soldiers went into the hut and returned a short while later with an officer. This military officer approached us in an extremely belligerent manner. He looked us over and in a harsh voice told us that we were now officially Czechoslakian Prisoners of War ("Vojenski Zajatcy in Czech"). Although neither of us was fluent in Czech, we knew exactly what he meant.

I felt numb from the anger that was building within me as I realized that once again we had been betrayed. Czechoslovakia had not declared war on Poland and we had not been captured on some battlefield, nor were we in possession of any arms while in their country. To compound my anger, the officer said that if we tried to escape, the guards were under orders to shoot to kill. We had left one country that had reneged as an ally, but that did at least provide some shelter, to come to another country that claimed to be neutral but then interned us as prisoners of war without any declaration of war or threat on our part.

The attitude of the guards now became hostile. We were immediately taken into an anteroom in the headquarters building for questioning. Once the questioning was completed, we were escorted to the barracks that were to be our accommodation. The compound appeared to have previously been a military camp and barracks. There were a number of barrack buildings that were in fact large rooms. Each of these rooms accommodated up to fifty prisoners. The beds for the prisoners were placed, almost touching, around the exterior walls. In the centre was a wood heater, to provide and maintain some warmth in the barracks during winter. We were certainly crowded in as tightly as possible.

Each barrack was under the control of a senior non-commissioned officer (NCO), such as as a sergeant, who was also a prisoner. This NCO reported to a Czech Officer and the Czech military guards when necessary. He would also pass down any orders or rules and regulations issued by the camp commander. We were not permitted to approach any of the Czech officers or guards, except through this NCO. In charge of my barracks was a sergeant from a Polish cavalry unit.

There were already a number of Poles in the barrack. Like us, all had been captured while trying to return home. I did not meet any POWs from the same internment camp that I had left a few days ago. These men had come from other Hungarian internment camps. This only confirmed to us that the Hungarians were fully collaborating with the Nazis and had set up their internment camps around the time of the German invasion.

Both the accommodation and the food we received were of an acceptable standard. We now had beds to sleep on and blankets with which to keep warm, particularly now that winter was quickly arriving. Over the last few months, we had slept wherever we could, with only the clothes we wore to keep warm. Sleeping on and under straw as we did in Hungary was a luxury, quickly surpassed when we received a bed and blanket. The food was adequate and quite edible. We often had what the Czechs called "nudlieczki", a food similar to dumplings. I found these to be very appetizing and became quite fond of nudlieczki during my time at that camp.

The snows came early in 1939, well before the arrival of winter proper. The Czechs began to use the prisoners to clear the snow from the surrounding roads, particularly after heavy snowfalls. We were organised into gangs and each morning were escorted to some sites where the snow needed to be cleared. This was indeed hard work. Although most of us were fairly fit, we had to work outside in the elements. There were no additional clothes such as coats, gloves or snow boots provided, even on the coldest of days. The guards did not accept that the inhospitable conditions meant that we could not work at a pace they imagined we should. They did not want to be out in the sleet or freezing snow and would quickly show their displeasure at anyone whom they thought was keeping them there for any longer than necessary.

As with any group of prisoners, some began talking about escaping to get home for Christmas. There was always someone who had an escape plan for a small group or someone with a plan for a mass escape in the style of the film "The Great Escape". These plans were discussed, dissected, evaluated and discussed again. Most plans were no more than wishful thinking, particularly now that the winter weather had set in. Anyone who could get out of the compound without being shot would almost likely freeze to death out in the woods before they got very far. Those who escaped and were recaptured would most likely be shot. The chances of a successful escape were negligible.

I had been at the compound only a short time when our cavalry sergeant informed us that he had been approached by one of the Czech officers with an offer. The officer had apparently told the sergeant that he was aware of the plans and talk of escaping, and that for a price he was prepared to help. He claimed that he could show any escapees how to reach the main gate where a soldier, who had been bribed, would open the gate and let them escape. The escapees would be gone well before any of the other guards were aware that they were missing but, once outside the gate, he couldn't help them any further and they would be on their own. The price for his help was all the watches, rings and any other valuables that the escaping prisoners owned.

The officer's proposal did create some interest amongst some groups of prisoners. There was some concern that there may be a Czech mole within our ranks, as the officer had said that he was aware of our plans. In reality the officer could say that with confidence because escape plans would most likely be discussed within any group of prisoners. Most of the escapes that we could dream up had probably been tried before, both at this compound and elsewhere.

The escape proposal was mulled over and over by a particular group of prisoners. I was against the proposal from its inception and said so. I argued that I could smell a rat in the plan and it was likely to be a setup. The thought that any prisoner would hand over all his valuables suggested to me that he would not need them where he was going. I refused to be a party to this escape plan and some others joined me. We were ignored by the group and they kept planning and scheming. The sergeant agreed to act as their go-between for the arrangements with the officer. A month or so later, six of the prisoners agreed terms with the Czech officer. The date and time for the escape was arranged and the valuables duly handed over.

Over the next few days, there was an air of expectation among those prisoners who had some involvement in the escape. Most of the inmates in our barrack knew of the initial approach and most realised that there was a group who were very interested. Few knew of the final arrangements, but an escape would not have been a surprise to anyone. Everyone involved had to be extremely careful not to let anything slip or to cause any suspicions with the Czech guards. At the appointed time the men set off, following the officers directions. As they approached the main gate all the searchlights were suddenly illuminated. This caught them out in the open and with nowhere to go. The machine gunners on the towers began firing and did not stop until every body was riddled with bullets. As many of us had feared, the approach was just a ruse to get their hands on the prisoners' valuables. The loss of lives was inconsequential to the Czech officer and the guards, who all seemed to enjoy their part in the slaughter of six men. The bodies were quickly removed and disposed of by the guards, leaving only the blood stains in the snow and on the ground as a reminder of what some men are capable of doing. I believe that there is a God and I pray that the men responsible for this inhumanity pay dearly for the rest of eternity.

The murders of unarmed prisoners sent a shock wave through the camp. There was nothing anyone could do. There was no higher authority to whom we could appeal and the Czech officer immediately denied any complicity or knowledge of the escape and the murders. The disquiet within the camp meant that the guards became more on edge and punishment was meted out for even the smallest infraction of the rules. After a few weeks, the routine in the camp slowly began to return to normal. The plans and talk of proposed escapes that had been put aside for a while began to resurface. The raising of escape ideas, the discussion and the planning were an important part of prisoners' lives and helped them overcome many adversities that were part and parcel of incarceration. However, we had been taught a harsh lesson and we would never again trust anything uttered by a camp officer.

In early December, we heard a rumour that we were to be sent home for Christmas. I do not know how the rumour started, but it went around the compound very quickly. Many of us suspected that it was not true, and it did turn out that way as we spent our first Christmas in the compound as prisoners. Even with Christmas approaching, there was no change in our routines. Unfortunately, nor was there any roast turkey and dumplings served to us at lunch on Christmas Day.

The New Year passed without any fanfare. A day or so later we received orders from the Czech commandant that all the prisoners had to prepare to leave the compound. We were told that we were finally going home. Preparations did not take long as our meager possessions consisted of some additional underwear and possibly a spare shirt. The Czechs had been good enough to occasionally supplement our meagre wardrobe. These possessions were carried in our little "bread" bag. Some of the men were able to scrounge some food from within the compound to take with them. We were assembled and, some time around midday, marched under heavy escort to a railway station located about 3 kms away from the compound. I had seen the station before, when we had cleared snow from the roads in that area. The march to the station was rather difficult and extremely tiring. There had been heavy snowfalls the previous day and night and the roads had not been cleared. The weather was extremely cold and all we had to keep us warm was the clothes we were wearing.

As we approached the station, I could see that there was a train already there waiting. The train consisted of the engine, a large number of cattle wagons and one passenger wagon, located at the end. It was obvious that there were too many prisoners for us all to fit into the passenger wagon, so that wagon was likely to be for the guards.

We were marched onto the platform and halted. We were ordered to stand to attention and then, as if from nowhere, a group of soldiers, in German uniform, appeared and approached our column. This was our first sighting of German soldiers in Czechoslovakia.

Our suspicions of collaboration were now shown to be fact. After a brief exchange of words between the German officers and the Czech guards, the guards marched off, leaving us with the Germans. One of the German officers turned to us and announced in Polish that we were now German prisoners of war. Anyone trying to escape would be shot like a dog.

With the formalities completed, we were ordered to board the cattle wagons. Each wagon was filled to its absolute capacity so there was standing room only. We were wedged in so tightly that there was insufficient room for anyone to sit or lie down. It was impossible to fall as everyone was holding each other up. Once the wagons were loaded, the doors were locked with padlocks and the train moved off on what turned out to be a long and very inhospitable journey. After travelling for about twenty-four hours, the train stopped in the city of Wroclaw. We were now in Poland, our homeland. We had traveled in freezing conditions for the last twenty-four hours and our only warmth was that generated by the closeness of our bodies. The wagons had no heating, nor were they insulated against the weather. We had not been provided with any food or drink and we had also been forced to stand for the entire journey.

After our arrival at Wroclaw in the morning, the train remained closed up and just stood at the station. I would guess the temperature to have been around minus 20 degrees Fahrenheit in the wagons. This was typical for this part of Europe in the depths of winter. It was so cold that I wondered if they were trying to freeze us to death. Sometime that afternoon the German soldiers surrounded the train, unlocked the wagon doors and pulled them open.

Some people, who turned out to be Red Cross personnel, had been permitted to approach the train and provide us each with some hot coffee and a sandwich. This was the first meal and warm drink that we had received since the breakfast we had had before marching out of the prison compound in Czechoslovakia. The coffee and food helped to warm us up a little and the brief respite from the cramped conditions enabled us to sit and stretch our bodies and limbs.

During mid-afternoon, we were ordered from the train, assembled and marched to another train at the station. And so another train journey began. We were packed into the same type of carriages and had identical traveling conditions. The Germans did not provide any more food or drink, so we would have to survive on the food provided by the Red Cross earlier that day. This time we were heading west and we guessed that the next stop would be somewhere in Germany. After traveling all night in freezing and inhospitable conditions, we arrived at the town of Landsdorf, early the next morning. We were now in Germany.

THIS SOLDIER'S FORTUNE

9

Germany

With typical German efficiency, it seemed that as soon as the train stopped it was immediately surrounded by German soldiers. The doors were unbolted and thrown open and our disembarkation commenced immediately. Few of us could speak German and few Germans could speak Polish, but we were left in no doubt as to what they wanted by their gestures, incessant yelling and physical abuse. We were assembled into a column and counted off. Then we began the march from the railway station to the prisoner of war camp that was to be our new home.

Along the way, we were quite often verbally abused and threatened by some German youth as we passed by. I suspect that they did not like the fact that we Poles were the first to oppose Hitler and his war machine, even though we were really no match for them at that time. The guards would not permit them to get too close to us and controlled their antics quite well. Others, particularly the older people, just looked at us without any enmity or pity in their eyes. It seemed that we were simply prisoners to them and not worth them concerning themselves about.

The POW compound was located on the outskirts of the town, near a large cemetery. This cemetery was the final resting place of many prisoner,s from many nationalities, who had died in the compound after their capture, mainly during WW1. It also now contained a number of deceased Polish prisoners of war from WW2. There were many more yet to be buried in this cemetery during and after the time of my internment there.

The compound where we were was vast, but still typical of any major compound. It was enclosed by two tall, barbed wire fences and outside those fences were guard towers, with machine guns, manned by uniformed German soldiers. The towers were sited to provide clear sight of the fences as well as interlocking fields of fire for their weapons. We had no doubts that the guards would not hesitate to use their weapons as had already been demonstrated to us in Czechoslovakia. As additional security, guards leading large and savage looking guard dogs constantly patrolled the perimeter fences. The entrance to the compound was through a large gate that was guarded by more soldiers. Any person or vehicle entering or departing the compound was thoroughly checked and monitored. We did not know it at the time, but this compound was actually only a transit camp where prisoners were assembled, before being assigned and dispatched to other POW camps (Stalags) elsewhere in Germany.

Once we had marched into the camp, we were quickly and efficiently registered and given a prisoner number. My number was 9306 Stalag X11C. The 9306 was my POW number and the X11C signified the prisoner of war compound in which I was interned.

The compound comprised a number of large

buildings. Some were used for administration, some for prisoner accommodation and the rest as kitchens and storerooms. There were also some old stables that were not being used at the time. I estimated that there were several thousand prisoners at the compound when I arrived, a number that did not vary much at any time. This number of prisoners was far more than could be accommodated within the barrack buildings, so the compound yard was dotted with an innumerable number of small two-man tents for additional accommodation. Some of the men were assigned to the barracks, but by the time they got to me there was no space left. All of the other new arrivals, myself included, were assigned to the two-man tents. Each tent was a basic canvas shelter with some straw thrown onto the bare earth floor. My tent-mate and I received one blanket to share. There was no heating, lighting or any other amenities. This was to be our home for a number of weeks until something better eventually became available.

We found the food to be almost inedible and of little or no nutritional value. Breakfast consisted mainly of a "mush" similar to very watery gruel or porridge. Lunch was the main meal of the day and often consisted of weak fish soup with little or sometimes no vegetables. This soup usually contained just the heads and tails of the fish but little or no flesh. If we were really lucky it might also contain some maggots. We eventually came to regard maggots as just another source of protein that most other ingredients lacked. For the evening meal we might receive a slice of bread made from some mixed milled grains. Even though many of us had been farmers, we could not always identify all of the grains used in baking the bread. I am sure that the Germans themselves would not eat the food they provided to us. They saw us merely as prisoners and we didn't warrant anything better. From my later personal experiences and observations, the Germans we captured were always treated with more respect and provided with far better food and accommodation than many probably deserved. Our standards for them were far higher than anything that we were ever afforded.

The winter weather continued to remain bitterly cold and these conditions devastated many poor souls, particularly those living in the tents. Daily temperatures were still in the minus range and reached as low as minus 20 degrees celsius or lower during the night. The prisoners housed in the barracks were fortunate to be in a proper enclosed building that had a fire to provide some warmth, at least for part of the night. Survival for the prisoners living in the tents was a different matter. It was up to us to find ways of keeping warm. My tent-mate and I developed a routine where we would snuggle together, as closely as possible, to warm up one side of our bodies. Once we had warmed up one side we would quickly change sides to warm up the other side. This routine was followed quite often each night and, although it interrupted our sleep, it enabled us to alternatively warm up both sides of our bodies and maintain some all round body warmth.

Many of the injured, sick and weak perished under such intolerable conditions. Every morning soldiers would come around and remove the bodies of those poor prisoners who had frozen to death or just simply gave up and died during the night. Even the fitter and healthier men struggled to survive. It was impossible for anyone to remove their boots and what was left of their socks, as there was the constant possibility of getting frostbitten. Each man understood this danger and had to pay particular attention to his hands, feet and face. Frostbite could easily lead to gangrene and at that time there was no effective treatment or medication for this affliction. There was only amputation.

For most prisoners there was little to do within the compound. However, there was work outside the compound in the forms of road clearing, gathering wood for the kitchens and heating, or cutting down trees to be made into lumber. The compound was not built to accommodate the number of prisoners being held there, so there was also a need for a rapid building program. The healthier and fitter men were organised into work gangs and marched out under an armed escort, to work on one of these tasks. For the rest of the men, until the building program came into full swing, their daytime was taken up trying to keep warm and finding ways to pass the time. Once sufficient lumber had been cut and prepared, gangs of prisoners were put together to erect new barrack buildings. The two-man tents were being removed and replaced by wooden buildings. Hopefully, no more men would need to endure the hardships of a winter living in tents.

We also came across a problem that we had not previously encountered. Lice were in plague proportions at this compound, surviving even in the freezing conditions. The Germans themselves were very concerned as their men were also infested with this vermin. At one time the camp doctor decided to study this plague and to obtain specimens. He offered a slice of bread to anyone who could bring him large, live louse. There were people lined up outside his office each day waiting to exchange a louse for a slice of bread.

Conditions began easing somewhat with the arrival of spring and the gradual improvement in the weather. In the three months that I existed in Stalag X11C (it is hard to describe it as "lived"), I had lost fifteen kilos of weight. It would be some time before I regained any of my previous weight and strength. I also saw the departure of many men to other Stalags situated throughout Germany, and the arrival of many more men who were yet to experience and live through true Nazi hospitality.

My existence improved somewhat when I was in a group of prisoners assigned to leave our two-man tents and relocate into the previously empty stables. The stables were not used during the winter months. If they had been, some of the unfortunate souls who suffered and died from the cold might have survived. Living conditions in the stables were spartan but still a long way ahead of living in tents. The stable floor was made of concrete and was lightly covered with straw for insulation. The straw was also our mattress at night. To fit everyone in, we were required to lie side by side on the floor to sleep. Anyone who got up in the night found that the space they left had been quickly filled by the movement of sleeping bodies. They were then left trying to find another place where they might be able to squeeze into.

Near the end of March 1940, I was informed that I was being transferred to another Stalag. Without any further fanfare or delay, all those to be transferred were formed into a column and escorted to the railway station. My stay at Stalag X11C lasted almost three months, from very early in January 1940 to almost the end of March. The depths of winter had now turned to spring and the weather was beginning to improve. We could only hope that where we were going would be better than where we had been.

10

Stalag V111B

We were packed into waiting carriages and the train departed. On this trip, we were transported in passenger carriages. Everything was done quickly, with the Germans making sure that anyone dilly-dallying was punished and brought into line. Again, we were not provided with any supplies of food or water before we left nor during the remainder of our trip. Conditions were once again cramped, but I was fortunate enough to climb up onto on overhead luggage rack and keep out of the crush. I remained on the rack for the entire journey, lasting nearly forty-eight hours. The effects of our malnutrition, the cramped conditions and the lice that we all carried continued to make our lives a misery.

The train finally stopped at a town called Limburg, located in the south-west of Germany, some 50 kms from the French border. We were quickly disembarked from the train and escorted to the awaiting Stalag. Most of the prisoners could now understand the instructions being barked at us in German and some prisoners could even speak a little of the language. This was of considerable assistance to us as we could quickly comply with the guards' instructions, thereby avoiding them becoming angry and frustrated. This saved more than one prisoner from receiving a blow to the head or back with a rifle butt. The guards were not particular where or how they hit us. All they wanted was maximum effect on the prisoners.

I was now imprisoned in Stalag V111B. The POW number that was issued to me at the previous Stalag remained, but the Stalag number changed. The set up of this Stalag was very similar to the one we had just left, with the barbed wire, guard towers and so on. The advantage of this Stalag, as far as we prisoners were concerned, was that it had more barrack huts for our accommodation. Even if it was spring and warmer, we dreaded the thought of living in tents again. Overall, our new accommodation in Stalag V111B was a considerable improvement. The standard of the food was even marginally better. Breakfast was still the gruel or porridge and for the midday meal we were still served soup or a watery stew. However, this was improved with the regular addition of some meat and vegetables. A slice of bread was still the staple for the evening meal.

The Stalag rules and regulations were the same as in the previous Stalag, and the dire penalties for any infringements were again spelt out to us. A week or so after our arrival, we were all photographed, from the front and then from both sides. These photographs were for our POW records. We were also informed that we were forbidden to have any relationships with any German women. There was no defence for such fraternisation, even if the woman was willing and actively encouraged the relationship. This was a crime for which there was only sentence, death by hanging. This sentence would be imposed without a trial and there were no rights of appeal. We were forced to sign a written acknowledgement that this had been explained to us and that we understood the consequences. This acknowledgement actually provided the Nazis with complete power of life or death over us. Anyone could be accused, found guilty and summarily executed, even if the accusation was false or could not be proven. I later heard that some prisoners had been executed under this law. However, I do not know whether the cases were factual or whether the accusations were true or false. There was nothing that we could do about this. Prisoners had no rights or legal standing under Nazi law.

Camp life changed very little. Guards still watched us from their towers while manning their machine guns. All the fit men were still required to work within the camp and out in the surrounding forest. There was always the need to log trees for timber and to satisfy the firewood requirements of the camp. We were still assigned to work gangs and escorted to our work areas each day.

After a couple of weeks in Stalag V111B, the lives of many of its prisoners changed overnight. All prisoners who had been farmers or involved in farming activities prior to the war were formed into work gangs of thirty or so members. Each work gang was then sent to a small town or village within a short radius of the Stalag. A new chapter of my life was about to begin in a village called Guttenberg.

11

Guttenberg

The Nazis needed to replace the labour on their farms and agricultural facilities that was being lost by the conscription of German men into the war machine. They decided that they could cover these losses through the use of forced labour. There were already many thousands of prisoners of war interned in Stalags throughout Germany, many with the knowledge and experience to step in and fill the breach. To make their system operate efficiently, prisoners were assigned to work gangs of thirty men. The composition of each gang was made up of men with the knowledge and experience to meet the requirements of the area in which they would work. There were many such work gangs created, and each gang was sent to work on farms in a particular area. The gang to which I was assigned was sent to the village of Guttenberg.

We were billeted in a building that was once the village school. All thirty of us were accommodated in a large room that was previously a classroom. There was only one doorway into the room and that was kept bolted, with armed guards stationed outside (there was one armed guard for every ten prisoners). All windows were sealed and barred to prevent any escape. Each prisoner was assigned their own bunk bed, containing a rather thin mattress and one blanket. This was to be our "home" for the time we worked in the village.

The working arrangements, as explained to us, were that we would continue to be the responsibility of the military. However, we would only be under the direct supervision of the military from the time we returned from work each night until we were escorted to our place of work in the morning. The people who owned the businesses, or the farmers themselves, were responsible for us at all other times. They were authorised to shoot us if we either stole anything, tried to escape or attempted anything with the women. Each morning, the guards would escort each of us to our place of work. At the end of each day, the business owners or farmers would escort us back to the school for the night. All of our food requirements such as breakfast, midday and evening meals would be catered for at the workplace. They would also supply clothing and footwear when it was required. Nothing was available for the prisoners at the billet at the school.

I was assigned to work on a farm owned by Jacob Sijben. The work was hard, but most of the farmers were reasonable men and understood that the prisoners could not do any more than they themselves could do. The meals I received were the same as those that Jacob and his family ate. However, I was not permitted to eat with them at their table. This was one of the many regulations issued by the authorities. From my personal experience, most of the farmers would have been happy to invite their assigned workers into their homes. Most of us had learned some German and so we could converse with them. We could understood their problems and discuss them as well do our fair share of the work. After a short time, most of us gained their trust and, in a fashion, began to share their lives. My new life must have agreed with me because after a while I began to regain my full strength and replace some of the weight that I had lost at Stalag X11C.

This was now my life, twenty-four hours per day, seven days per week. It stayed this way throughout the remainder of 1940 and into 1941.

At some stage in 1941, our work gang was assembled for a meeting with some senior German Officers from the directorate responsible for the prisoner work scheme. They put to us a proposal that, according to them, would release us from being held and treated as prisoners of war. They wanted each prisoner to sign a form requesting a discharge from the Polish army. As the Nazis were the "government" in Poland, they could grant the discharges and we would be released from military service to become civilians. A condition of this proposal was that, even though we would no longer be prisoners of war, each of us had to live at the farm to which we had been assigned and continue to work there until the end of the war. Any time that we were not required to work would be our own. As an incentive, we would be paid for our work (in German Marks) and would be permitted to spend our money in the village. As civilian workers, we would be issued with identity papers that would allow us to live and travel within the town or locality. However, the law on fraternisation would continue to apply to us. Having put forward their proposal, they agreed to give us some time to consider it.

Discussions on this proposal began directly after the meeting and continued for some time without any consensus being reached. It was an issue that totally consumed us night after night. There were some who thought that the proposal was fair and reasonable and believed that the gang members should go along with it. They reasoned that it would free us from the military oversight that we had endured for more than twelve months. It would also provide us with some basic freedoms. On top of that, we would have some money to enjoy these freedoms. We could easily imagine ourselves going into the village to meet other people, buy some beer or schnapps, something to eat or even some clothes. Also, living on the farms would be much more preferable to coming back to our barrack room each night and then leaving for the farms each morning. This was the rationale being put forward by the people in favour of accepting the proposal.

My friend Stasiek (Stan) Tomaszewski and I were not in favour of the proposal. We argued, particularly with some of the pro-proposal members, that we should fully understand what the proposal was meant to achieve for the Nazis, and consider all the consequences, before signing the forms. Our view was that if we signed, most of the soldiers currently guarding our work gang, as well as many other guards with similar work gangs throughout Germany, could be transferred to other duties. We saw it as a scheme by which, for little cost, the Nazis would utilise our labour while at the same time reducing their commitment of both manpower and financial cost for guarding us. Therefore, by signing, we may be actually helping the Nazis to channel more manpower into their war effort and possibly help them win the war. These arguments raged back and forth. Some people immediately saw our point of view or were eventually convinced that we may be right. Others were not so sure but at least were not confident enough to sign their forms. Personally, I was pleased that the Nazis were being thwarted and that I was contributing to their problems. I may not have been able to fight them with a rifle or bayonet but I, and many others who thought as I did, could make it difficult for them to reach their goals.

The issue of accepting or not accepting their proposal eventually led to an impasse within members of our work gang. Some time had passed, but no-one from our work gang had signed or submitted their forms. Even the members who were for the proposal would not do so until we had all agreed. This caused much frustration and some anger among the military authorities. The guards were told to lean on us by making life a little uncomfortable and to make us see some Nazi common sense. I suspect that their reasoning was that if one or two signed, others would follow suit and also sign. This actually began to work against them and, despite the cajoling from the guards, we continued to resist their efforts.

It seems that the guards, possibly as a result of overhearing our discussions and occasional heated debate, had decided that I was one of the main culprits convincing the others not to sign the discharge forms. I suspect that I was singled out to be taught a lesson. One night, just as we were getting ready to turn in for the night, one of the guards came into our room. I was sitting at the foot of my bunk wearing only my shirt, work pants and socks. It was about 10 pm, the usual time that a guard would come in to check that we were all there before locking us in for the night. Tonight was different, because he came in holding his rifle with the bayonet attached. This was highly unusual and immediately raised our concerns. He kept walking around the room, swearing and yelling that tonight all of us were going to die. He continued his circling and then, as he approached my bunk, he screamed that there was one Polish swine who was going to die right then and there.

He charged at me with his rifle and bayonet leveled. In that instant I made a decision that was to save my life. I sidestepped the charge, grabbed the rifle from his hands and pushed him with all my strength to the floor. I then threw the rifle under the bunk and ran through the open door and down the steps into the guard's room. One of the other guards tried to stop me but I managed to push him out of the way and ran out of the building through the front door. Fortunately, the door was not locked, so I continued running to the front gate. When I tried to open the gate, I found that it was locked and so I leapt over a high stone wall that surrounded the building and onto a road. The level of the road was lower than the level of the school grounds and the fence had a drop of some 3 metres from the top to the road surface. To increase the height of the wall, there was a coil of barbed wire fastened to the top. Having overcome these obstacles, I leapt over a number of smaller fences, running through farmers' gardens and into the open fields.

I finally came to a stop in a forested area. I could not fully grasp nor comprehend everything that had just happened to me. I felt numb in mind and body and totally exhausted. I sat down under a tree and almost instantly fell asleep. I had heard that, in times of a personal crisis such as this, everything seems to happen in slow motion and that a person can get the strength of ten men. This is what had happened to me. I could avoid the bayonet charge because it was happening in slow motion, which provided me with the time to decide what to do and then act. Then I had the strength to grasp the rifle and to tear it out of my attacker's hands and knock him to the floor. I had the power to bodily barrel the other guard out of the way and then leap a high stone fence and drop 3 metres, land without hurting myself and then run and keep on running. Before this experience, I would never have believed that it was possible to do all that I had done.

When I woke in the morning, the sun was shining through the branches of the pine tree. It was the beginning of April 1941, early spring. There was a cool breeze, yet I was warm enough. I asked myself, "What am I doing here, under a pine tree, at this time of the morning? I should be at the farm and working." I stood up and looked around, wondering how I had come to be there. A pinecone dropped at my feet and I looked down to see that I was not wearing my boots. All I could see were my worn out old socks. I just stood for some time, trying to remember what had happened and how I had come to be standing in a forest without any boots on. Eventually, a little voice inside me whispered in my ear, "Zygmunt, you were nearly murdered last night by one of the guards but because of a split second decision to run, you are still alive." My memory began to return and the images in my mind of what had happened became graphically clear. The only thing that was not clear, and is still not clear to this day, is how I managed to leap a tall stone fence with barbed wire on the top and not get a scratch. It sounds like a fairy story, but it is true and it did happen to me.

My most immediate problem then was what I should do next. The consequences of what had happened began to dawn on me. I could not return to the school. By now I would have been reported as having escaped custody. The guard who attacked me would still be there and would no doubt want to finish what he had started. To compound my situation, I had attacked two guards in the course of making my escape. I presumed that this is the story that the guards would have told when reporting my escape. They were not likely to admit that I had escaped because one of them was trying to kill me. If the guards were looking for me and found me, it is likely that I would be executed on the spot. The guards would proudly drag my body back to show the others what happens when you defy them. There was a good chance that most of the prisoners would sign their forms under that pressure.

I sat under the pine tree and pondered my next step. Physically, I felt quite refreshed, but I was ravenously hungry. I came to the conclusion that escape from Germany was nearly impossible. I would need to travel right through Germany and, if I somehow managed that, would then be faced with travelling through neighbouring countries that were occupied by the Germans. All Germans, young and old, were told that if they saw any escaping prisoners they must report them or shoot to kill. I did not think that my chances of escape were realistic.

As I sat there I realised that I could hear the sounds of cars, not too far away. This suggested that there was a main road nearby. I decided to look around and get some bearings because I had no idea where I was. Approaching the road, I decided to walk beside it to see if I could recognize any landmarks that could pinpoint where I was. I recognized the area as being not far from the town of Krueznah. The headquarters of the military authorities responsible for all the prisoner work gang programs in this district were located there, and I had been to this headquarters once before whilst en route to Guttenberg.

What was I to do now? I had worked out where I was, but not what I was going to do. There were not many options available, and so I made another snap decision. I would report directly to the headquarters to surrender myself and state my case. Having made that decision, I headed down the main road and into town. There was now no turning back.

On the road there was a lot of traffic, both vehicular and pedestrian, heading in both directions. I passed some units of German soldiers marching up the road. They may have been on their way to search for me for all I knew. Even with all this movement, I could not believe my luck. Not one soldier or civilian took any notice of me. How could all of these people not notice someone dressed only in a shirt, work pants and socks walking down the road? Perhaps they just chose to ignore me. After walking for about an hour, I reached the town and walked up to the headquarters building. I had no real idea of what I was going to do or say now that I was there. This had been going through my mind while walking, but I still had not formulated a plan of what I would say. I could only hope for understanding and justice once I explained my reason for escaping from Guttenberg.

I entered the building, still unchallenged, and approached the office. I noticed that a door was open and inside the office I could see a German Officer, a captain. He was speaking rather loudly on the telephone and I understood him to say something to the effect of "He could not get far" and "Keep watch at the railway station and trains going east". I immediately thought that he was speaking about me. When he put the phone down, I approached the doorway, knocked and stood waiting. He turned and asked in sharp voice what I wanted. I told him that I was the prisoner he was looking for. His face did not show any surprise at what I had said, nor did his expression change as he came over and looked me up and down. He remained expressionless, with no indication in his face, eyes or body language as to what he was thinking. Suddenly, he burst out laughing. He said that I was not going to get very far dressed like that and without any shoes on my feet. He called me into the office and then demanded an explanation. I told him of the previous night's happenings as I remembered them. I explained that I was not escaping but ran to save my life and for that I did not deserve to be executed. He told me that he had been informed only that I had escaped from the farm.

The officer wrote down all that I told him. After a little while, he asked if I was hungry. I told him that I was (it was 2pm by this time and I had not eaten since the previous night). He stood and led me to a kitchen where he told the cook to prepare a good meal for me. This was far more than I ever could have hoped for or expected. Perhaps this was to be the last meal for a condemned man. I was very aware that if my story did not hold up there could be a firing squad waiting for me. ,

After I had finished eating, one of the soldiers brought me a pair of shoes. They were a reasonable fit and once I put them on he took me to a small room and said that I could rest there. The room contained only a bed and a chair. I laid down and tried to once again go over everything that had happened during the previous twenty-four hours and to somehow make some sense of it all. Before too long, I fell asleep, sleeping through what was left of the afternoon and the night. I woke only when the cook came in and called me for breakfast. I could not believe the respect and hospitality that I was receiving. Following breakfast, one of the soldiers came and escorted me to the captain's office. He called me in and I stood to attention in front of his desk. He looked at me and said that I would not be punished as he now knew the truth. At that moment, I realised that my instincts had been correct and I had made the right decision to come to the headquarters and turn myself in. For the first time, I saw an example of how good and just a German soldier could be. He had listened to me and considered my position and actions justly and with compassion. He was the first German soldier who treated me with respect and was not just brutal in words and deeds.

In hindsight, it is incredible what can happen to a person in such a short period of time. Someone had tried to murder me, I did things that I once would not have believed possible, I took a risk that could have resulted in exactly what the soldier was trying to achieve in the first place, and I met a German officer who was a decent human being. I am sure that there were many others like him, but I had only come into contact previously with those who were not. So much went right for me as well. Had I been challenged and captured by the soldiers on the road, I would have been thrown into jail. Once they found that I was an escapee, it would have been the end of me. How did I manage to walk into a military office unchallenged and meet the Captain? As luck would have it, his door was open and he happened to be in his office at the time. He then took the trouble to confirm my story, probably personally, because if he had left that to some subordinate they may have believed the guards' versions of the escape story.

I do not know what became of that guard in Guttenberg who tried to murder me, but I hope he got his just desserts. I also hope that the Captain survived the war and lived (or perhaps still lives) a good and happy life, for he was a good and decent man.

12

Meddersheim

To avoid any further problems with the soldiers and guards in Guttenberg, the headquarters reassigned me to the work gang in the village of Meddersheim, some 30 kms away from Krueznah. I was taken there in an army truck and left with the military guards responsible for the work gang. It seems that the guards were not aware of my recent history because I was treated as any transferee would be. This dispelled some major concerns that I had of possible mistreatment by the guards.

The accommodation for the Meddersheim work gang was a large double story house that had been taken over by the military. On the ground floor was a living area that included a kitchen area and a storeroom. Upstairs were three rooms that had probably been used as bedrooms by the former residents. The guards used the ground floor as an office and storage area, while all the prisoners were squeezed into the upper rooms. The windows were barred to avert any escape, so our only avenue for movement was up and down the stairs and through the office area. Overall it was tight, but as we were only there during the evenings and overnight, it was not so bad.

The work routines at Meddersheim were the same as at Guttenberg. I was assigned to work on a farm, owned by Karl Venter, which was located some distance from the town. The following morning, I was escorted to Karl's farm to begin my work. As usual, the guards escorted me to the farm and Karl took me back each night. Karl was a veteran of WW1 and had been seriously wounded in the fighting. The injury had left him with limited use of his right arm. That did not stop him, however, although it did slow him down. He had two sons, the eldest serving in the German navy at that time and the other son still too young to be conscripted. Unfortunately, in 1945, shortly before I was finally liberated, he was conscripted into the army. I do not know if Karl or any of his sons survived the war. However, during my time working with Karl, I learned that he had no love for Hitler or the Nazis.

Karl treated me like a human being and life on the farm settled down. We worked hard and many long hours when that was required. The authorities seemed to have given up on their push for us to sign our discharge application forms. There was also no further pressure from the guards. The whole episode just became a non-issue in the end. It is hard now to imagine that I was almost murdered because I opposed the signing of the forms. Perhaps, sufficient numbers of prisoners had already signed, removing the need for the guards to continue pressuring the rest of us.

After a while, I became quite friendly with my fellow gang members. We were all in the same boat but there were two men with whom I became particularly friendly. The three of us shared a common dream. We all looked forward to the time when we would be free and beyond the bonds holding us as prisoners. We would talk about freedom and what it meant to us. This eventually led to talk of the possibilities and chances of making a successful escape. After all, we were about 50 kms from France and only some 60 kms from Switzerland. We were young and full of our ideals and dreams.

In the Autumn of 1942, the three of us became convinced that we could successfully escape. This put in motion further planning and more discussions, before we got down to actually formulating some detailed escape plans. As France was under Nazi control, our destination had to be Switzerland. We took every opportunity to study the maps of the district on the walls of the guards' office. This attention to detail provided us with information such as what we could expect to find along the way - towns or villages, landmarks, roads and tracks, rivers and streams and so on. Having developed a plan, we then began to gather a secret cache of food. We estimated that it would take two or three days of walking to reach the Swiss border, and so we required sufficient food for at least two days. On the farms, we often worked without supervision from the farmers or their families, so there were opportunities for us to hide some food and then take it to our cache when the opportunity arose. Secrecy and stealth were extremely important so that our actions could not be seen as preparations for an escape. We discussed our individual farm work schedules each night, looking for the opportune moment.

Eventually an opportunity presented itself. We had waited for the day when the three of us would be working alone on our farms, but still in close proximity to each other. As luck would have it, we received an unexpected bonus. On the day we selected to begin the escape, we would not only be working in close proximity but also close to the forest through which we were planning to travel for our escape. I was to be working in a vineyard at the end of Karl's farm, while both of my friends were to work in nearby fields. Now that we decided the when, the how was simple. At a certain time we would just down tools, meet at a designated spot, retrieve our food cache and disappear into the forest to begin the escape. Like any other plan, ours could fall apart at any minute. One of the farmers could change his mind as to where we would be working that day or decide to work alongside one of us. To cover this eventuality, we also devised a very simple contingency plan. If one of us did not arrive at the meeting point, the others would return to where they were working, pick up their tools and resume work. We would then reschedule our escape for the next available opportunity.

Thankfully, everything went to plan. As the sun began to set, we each downed tools, collected our food caches, met as planned and then bolted for the forest. We anticipated that when we did not turn up for dinner in the evening, the farmers would think that something had happened to us. It was very unlikely that they would know or realise that three of us, each on a different farm, had not returned for dinner. Each farmer would then wait a while, in case we were just running a little late, before going out to look for us. Once we could not be found, the farmer would have to go into the village to report our disappearance. We estimated that this would give us two or three hours head start before any alarm was raised. Even then, some more time would pass before any proper search could be mounted and it would be nighttime before their search could begin.

Our flight to freedom went extremely well and during the first night we covered a fair distance. We were well pleased. With everything going so well, we were all becoming more confident of success. Each of us fully understood the risks associated with our venture, but the rewards were great. Once we got to Switzerland, we would be free to do whatever we wanted.

Travelling through the forest meant that we could easily stray from our bearings, particularly during the night. The small compass that I had been secretly carrying on me all this time enabled me to monitor and correct the direction of our travel. I guess that this made me a sort of leader of our group. As the sun rose next morning we found a good sheltered spot to rest and laid up for the day. We were deep inside the forest so we felt relatively safe from detection. The only possibility was that someone may accidentally stumble onto our position, but that eventuality seemed extremely remote.

During the afternoon, the weather turned and it became quite overcast and misty with some intermittent showers. The temperature dropped noticeably and it became quite uncomfortable in our resting spot. Rather than sit around, we decided to resume our travel. After travelling for a while, we reached the edge of the forest and halted. We knew that there was a distance of approximately 1 km to a main road. We had taken into account that this kilometer stretch of mainly open land was the last place where it was likely that we could be found and intercepted. Once we crossed that road, there was nothing but more forest all the way to the Swiss border. There was no way that we could go around the stretch of open fields interspersed with small clumps of trees.

It was now quite dark and had begun raining lightly. We thought that such conditions - the darkness and rain - were in our favour, so we set off for the road. We utilized the small wooded areas as extra cover whenever we could. By the time we reached the road, it was raining quite heavily. We again halted, slightly away from the road, and watched and listened. The moon was clouded over and provided very little light. Our night vision was very sharp and none of us could spot any movement or colour on or near the road or anywhere in the fields. As for sounds, all we could hear was the rain. We felt confident to continue, so we began to dash across the road to reach the forest on the other side.

As we reached the centre of the road, all hell broke loose. We were lit up like startled rabbits when the area was suddenly flooded with light. We froze for a split second before self preservation kicked in. A machine gun opened fire on us and suddenly our lives depended on us getting off the road and into cover. We ran for our lives, over the road and diving into the trees on the far side. In hindsight, it is amazing that none of us was killed or injured. For a short time there, we had been "Sitting Ducks".

We found ourselves lying face down in a creek beside the road. We were not aware beforehand that there was a creek there and we certainly hadn't heard it. The machine gun was lashing the air and the vegetation above us so we had nowhere to go. Our flight to freedom had come to a sudden and inglorious end.

Once the soldiers realised that we were not running any longer, they stopped firing and yelled for us to come out with our hands up. We were aware that we had just run out of options so we stood up in the water. At this point, I realised that it would be wise to dispose of the compass that I had been carrying all this time. I reasoned that if compass was found on me, I would very likely be regarded as the ringleader and organiser of the escape. My punishment would most likely be much harsher than it would be for the other two. As I rose from the creek, I let the compass drop back into the water. We came out dripping wet and with our hands in the air. As we got back to the road, we were quickly surrounded, searched and had our food packs confiscated. We each received a blow to the back with a rifle butt. Such treatment was expected as the Germans never failed to express their authority in such a manner. The blows hurt and we stumbled forward but managed to remain on our feet. We were determined to show them that we were not weak and could stand up to that sort of treatment.

A squad of the soldiers left the main group and marched us to a village about a kilometer away from where we had been captured. The marching was not easy as our backs were extremely sore, and the soldiers kept prodding us with their rifles when any of us slowed our pace or stumbled. As we approached the village a mob of Hitler Youth, the young Nazi supporters, came up to us and began yelling abuse. They demanded that the soldiers shoot the Polish swine. They knew that something had happened, having heard the machine gun firing. They had come out to see what had happened and then seen us being escorted in. The sergeant in charge of our squad told them, in no uncertain terms, that we were unarmed prisoners and that they should shut up and go about their business.

We were then marched to a building in the village, let down into the cellar and locked in. The cellar was entirely empty and once the soldiers left it was almost pitch black inside. The three of us sat down in our sodden clothes, leaned back against the concrete wall and just sat there. The cellar floor consisted of packed sand and was actually quite comfortable to sit on. We had hardly said a word up to this point, and despite everything we had been through during the previous hour, we all fell into a deep sleep very quickly.

At about 8:30 the next morning, two guards came down into the cellar. The three of us were still in a type of light slumber when they came in, so they raised their voices and prodded our feet to bring us back to full consciousness. The guards ordered us up and, without saying anything further, escorted us upstairs to an administration office. Once inside the office, we were told to line up in front of the desk and stand to attention. There was a military officer (a Second Lieutenant) sitting behind the desk, with a secretary positioned close by. The secretary was holding a notebook and appeared ready to take notes of the upcoming proceedings.

One of the guards informed the officer that we were the escapees from Meddersheim. The officer stood up from behind the desk and came up to me. His face was expressionless and I had no idea as to what to expect. I was quite concerned that our captors might have been able to obtain my prisoner record during the night. That record might contain a reference to my pseudo-escape. With this current escape also taken into account, I could be in major trouble. The officer looked at me and demanded to know why I had tried to escape. I answered that I was a prisoner of war and wanted to escape to get my freedom back. It became obvious that he was not aware of my record, as he did not question me further. The officer then turned to the secretary and all he said was "Ten days". He turned to the others, looked at each and repeated, "Ten days". He made no attempt to ask either of them why they had tried to escape. We each wondered to ourselves what "Ten days" meant, but it was not long before we were to find out.

Once our sentence had been pronounced, the guards marched out of the office and we were taken out to the front of the building. There we waited until a truck arrived and we were ordered on board. Our guards also boarded and we were on our way. We had not travelled for long before the truck stopped outside a large farm building. I recognized the area to be near a small town called Sobernhaim. We were ordered off the truck and immediately ushered into the building. On entering, I noticed that inside the building were a number of lockable cells that were probably once pigsties. I whispered to my partners that it looked as if we had been assigned new jobs, looking after pigs. As we approached the first cell door, one of the guards opened it and I was forcibly pushed inside. The door was slammed shut and immediately locked. I then realised that I was mistaken. We were not going to look after pigs, but we were to be the pigs. I then understood the meaning of "Ten days". That was the length of our sentence in solitary confinement. Each of my friends was incarcerated in his own cell.

The inside of the cell was quite dim. There were no windows, just some ventilation vents high up near the roof. The vents provided some air circulation and allowed a little light into the cell. The cell was approximately 2 metres wide, 3 metres long and about 3 metres high. All four walls were made of stone and were about a metre thick. This solid construction meant that the inside temperature remained fairly constant both day and night. The floor was made of concrete and had some built-in drainage channels. The floor and walls were clean and fortunately did not harbour any bad smells or aromas. The lack of a window confirmed that I was in some sort of solitary confinement but, being an enterprising young fellow, I found that if I stood hard up against the inside wall, I could get a glimpse of the sky through the air vent. This might not sound like much, but when that is your only view of the outside world, it is everything.

Apart from their thermal qualities, the thick walls also permitted almost no sounds to penetrate in or out of the cell. I assumed that there was some movement of guards around the building and the cells, however I could not hear or see them. If a guard wanted to check on me or inspect the cell, he would need to open the door and come inside. As we were in solitary confinement, there was only one visit, which took place each morning.

Furnishings in the cell were indeed spartan. There was a single bed with only 3 planks across the base at about half a metre apart. There was no mattress and only one blanket. It was obvious that the guards did not care where or how we slept. Toilet facilities comprised a bucket standing in one corner. That was all well and good, but the problem was that no-one came to empty the bucket. It stood there until I realised that I was meant to tip the contents of the bucket down the drainage channel. This was not very sanitary or hygienic, but there was no other option. The Germans were soon to solve this problem for me quite effectively.

The next day seemed fine and sunny and the additional light coming through the vents brightened up my cell a little. This provided me with the opportunity to have a good look around. High up on the outside wall, I noticed what appeared to be a loose stone. It was only due to the extra light that I could see it, because in the normal gloom it was not so evident. I reached up and the stone came out easily. I put my hand into the cavity and felt something like rope or cord inside. I picked it out and found that there were some lengths of strong cord hidden inside. Someone who had been interned here before me must have smuggled the cords in and then left them there for use by later inhabitants such as myself.

Having these cords was one thing, but knowing what to do with them was another. The night before, while sleeping on the floor wrapped up in the blanket, I had the idea that I could fashion myself a hammock to sleep in. I took out the few loose planks from the bed frame and tied the corners of the blanket onto the frame. Once the blanket was stretched out and securely tied, it made a nice base to lie on. That night I had my first good night's sleep in the cell.

Had the guards found out that I had lengths of cord, they would have been confiscated very quickly and I would have been punished. To avoid discovery, I had to return the cords to their hiding place each morning before the guard came in. As the sun was rising, I would quickly dismantle my hammock, return the cords to their hiding place and replace the boards onto the bed frame. Each evening, after we had our day's final guard check, I would take out the cords and again prepare my bed. To be candid, I relished the thought that I had something that the Germans did not know about. It gave me a sense of "power". As long as I and others were careful to keep the cords concealed from the guards, future prisoners of this cell may experience this as well.

In solitary confinement, a day's rations amounted to one bottle of cold water and one slice of dry bread, about 2 centimetres thick. This would be brought in each morning by the guard when he came in to check that I was still alive and hadn't escaped. This ration provided my breakfast, lunch and dinner, all rolled into one slice. I quickly came to understand what living on bread and water alone really meant. After a few days there was no longer much need for the bucket in the corner.

The hardest part of being locked up for twenty-four hours each day is the boredom. There was nothing to do, nothing to see and no-one to talk to. The only noise that I could hear was the noise that I made myself as the thick walls kept any noise from the outside to a minimum. What little I could hear was unintelligible anyway. I could not communicate with or see any of the other prisoners. There were no sessions in an exercise yard where I might see and hear the outside world. My world consisted of a living space within four stone walls, with only a little light filtering in from above. To keep from going mad I often prayed, sang songs and recited nursery rhymes to myself. Living in that dark and gloomy environment could easily be soul destroying unless you were able to remain mentally strong and rational enough to keep your mind active. To compound my discomfort, the floor drains and the bucket really began to smell after a few days. The drains should have been hosed out but that was not going to happen, at least not while I was there. Before I was released from the cell I began getting used to it, but by then everything smelt the same.

All of a sudden, my ten days of confinement were over. It seemed to have taken so long to get to that point. One morning the guard came into the cell and told me to come out. As I emerged from this pig sty, I felt suddenly ill. The fresh air was not something that I was used to anymore and the light hurt my eyes, causing me to squint and causing tears to roll down my cheeks. My eyes would have only been slits as they struggled to adjust to all this daylight. I stood there trying not to collapse and trying to become accustomed to the outside world again. Once my composure had returned, I looked around the yard. My two escape partners had also been brought out and were going through the same adjustments as I was.

I could see one of the guards standing a little distance away from us and standing beside him was Karl Venter. Karl told me later that he had been informed of my recapture and had gone to the district headquarters to make enquiries about what was going to happen to me. He was concerned that I might be shot for escaping. They told him that I had been imprisoned and also when I was to be released. He requested that I be released into his custody and returned to work at his farm. My good fortune continued with that request being approved. Karl was there now, waiting to take me back to the farm. I do not know what happened to my two friends. They were not fortunate enough to have someone like Karl wanting them to return. After our release, they did not return to the Meddersheim work gang and I never saw either of them again.

I was now formally released into Karl's custody. We climbed onto his horse and cart and headed back to the farm. We didn't speak very much on the return journey, but I could see that he was concerned about the gaunt and pale way I looked. I had lost considerable weight in the two weeks since he last saw me. When we arrived at the farm, he said to me, "Zygmunt, stay here, you will be safe. We do not win the war and the first thing to do is get you back into shape". I will never forget these words as they were said from the heart. He then provided me with some washing facilities, some clean clothes and, most importantly, something to eat. I had not eaten a proper meal since the day of my escape and only had one slice of bread and water each day since being recaptured.

Then and there, I decided that I would accept this good man's advice and remain at his farm. That evening Karl escorted me back to my overnight accommodation in the town. I was a celebrity with the men whom I knew before my escape. They wanted to know everything about the escape, how we were recaptured and what happened after that. Celebrity status only lasts so long and before long my life as a prisoner returned to normal.

The guards showed little animosity and continued to treat me well. It was not long before the escape of three prisoners became a non-issue with them. Also, after a while, my relationship with Karl began returning to the level that existed before my escape. It was not a subject that we discussed. Karl knew that I would not attempt another escape because I had given him my word. Even still, I think he understood why I had tried.

13

Rebellion

As the war progressed, more and more German citizens, of all ages, were being pressed into military service. We were therefore required to work longer and harder, to produce more. We were now working upwards of fifteen hours a day, seven days a week. We all understood that this situation would most likely become worse if the war continued to go badly for the Germans. This was a matter of great concern to us as we became more and more affected. It became the subject of discussion amongst all the prisoners at every opportunity. Although there were also many times when we were too tired to worry about anything but sleep.

Our work gang consisted mostly of Poles and we were all Catholics. Most Poles were quite religious and would observe the religious days as well as Sundays whenever they could. Some of the prisoners raised the issue of not working on Sundays with their farm owners. This raised considerable concern amongst these farmers, particularly about what may happen next. To be fair to them, the farmers worked as hard as we did and were being given impossible production targets to meet. While being sympathetic to our cause, there was nothing that the farmers could do.

We became so concerned that we decided to approach our Guard Commander with a request that we be released from work on Sundays. We may not have been able to attend church services, but at least we could have a day of rest.

The Guard Commander was approached by a delegation of prisoners on a Saturday evening. He was informed that we would not be going to work the next day and that we now wanted every Sunday off work. I am not sure how seriously he took our request at that time. The next morning, we refused to get out of our beds. In a fashion, we had gone on strike - long before strikes became fashionable in Europe. The guards did not threaten or badger or try to force us to get up or go to work. Instead, the Guard Commander rang his commanding officer and informed him of the situation. We were then told to get up and assemble in the front yard of the house to await the arrival of the commanding officer.

We waited there for nearly two hours before the officer and an interpreter from the district headquarters arrived. The officer immediately demanded an explanation for our behaviour. This was not something that happened in the district before and the officer seemed quite unsure of what to do next. The interpreter spoke with us and then explained to the officer that we did not want to work on Sundays and our reasons for this. Most of us spoke German, but in situations such as this it was wise for both sides to use an interpreter. The officer looked at us as if he had been thunderstruck, staring at us with piercing eyes. When we did not show any signs of backing down, he said loudly that we were lucky that the Vermacht (the German army) did not send the SS to deal with us. If this had happened, we would all have been stood up against a wall and shot. That was the SS way of dealing with problems such as this, while at the same time setting a precedent for anyone else with similar ideas. He then threatened us that if we continued to refuse to work, beginning tomorrow (Monday), every tenth man in our work gang would be taken outside, lined up against the wall and shot. This would happen everyday until we went back to work or we had all been shot. He went on to say that if we immediately agreed to return to work, our work gang would be granted a half-day holiday every Sunday afternoon. He told us to discuss this between ourselves and to give him our answer very quickly.

We discussed his proposal amongst ourselves and quickly agreed that we would accept the half-day of rest, particularly as there was no penalty or trade-off required by the officer. We reasoned that, just as on the farms back home, there was always some work, such as milking or chopping firewood, that needed to be done on Sunday mornings. We informed the interpreter that we agreed to the proposal and would be returning to work on Monday. We were all quite pleased with the compromise. We had achieved something for our efforts. I do not know if any other work gang in Germany received such a concession. Once our euphoria settled, we realised that we had had nothing to eat for the day. There would be nothing until we returned for breakfast with the farmers on Monday morning.

The guards took us to the farms again on Monday morning and life quickly returned to normal. We continued to work hard, with fifteen hour days, but at least we would now get some respite. I did not know what Karl thought of our half Sunday off, but he didn't object or make an issue of it. The half-day proved to be a bonus for us. During the hot summer months, we arranged with the guards to go down by the river after we finished work. We would lie around on the riverbank, swim and wash our clothes on these fine afternoons.

There was one job on the farm that was particularly arduous. This was a job reserved for prisoners. Most of the farmers had vineyards and, in early spring and autumn, the soil around the vines needed to be fertilized. This was done by spreading animal manure around the vines. The manure was carried on our backs in containers weighing up to 50 kilograms. The vineyards were normally located on slopes, so we had to walk up and down these slopes spreading the fertilizer at the foot of each vine. On the positive side, at harvest time we were permitted to eat as many grapes as we wanted.

The harvesting of the grapes was another back-breaking job, as each cluster of grapes was cut from the vine by hand and placed into a basket. The basket was then carried along until it was full. Full baskets were emptied into a large container on a cart that was then pulled back to the house. This cycle of collecting the bunches of grapes continued until all the grapes had been harvested. This type of work was particularly hard on the hands and back, and needed a high level of fitness if we were to avoid major injury. Most farmers had their own equipment and skills to make their own wines. The wine was something that most prisoners, together with the farmers and their families, enjoyed with their meals.

Most of us prisoners had long since decided that it would be best to stay where we were in the hope of being liberated. Our chances of escape became more and more remote as German troops were starting to retreat back towards the fatherland. Anyone now captured escaping would probably be handed over to the SS and most likely be executed. Liberation was our only real hope now.

There was a real sense developing that the war would be over soon. Each night we would discuss amongst ourselves what we had seen and heard during that day. Often the farmers would say something about what they had read or heard. Occasionally, one of the prisoners would bring a newspaper back with them and someone, usually me, would translate any articles on the war. Some of the farmers had radios and so the transmissions would often be overheard. By keeping our eyes and ears open, we could glean all manner of useful information.

As evidence of what we had come to believe, there were increasing numbers of British and American fighters and bombers flying over Germany. There seemed to be little resistance from the famed Luftwaffe, the German air force. Allied fighters could be seen searching for targets during the day. The bombers could be heard both night and day and they left contrails in the sky as they flew over. Sometimes, we could hear allied bombing raids, particularly at night, when they operated nearby. This made us happy, to know that the German war machine was being destroyed, as well as confident that our liberation was at hand.

14

Liberation

On 12th March 1945, the American forces began their advance into Germany. All of those German forces once located in the extreme south were retreating to the north side of the river Rhine, near the town of Wiesbaden. They were establishing defensive positions all along the river, to keep the Americans from advancing any further into Germany. We prisoners were not aware of the advance until much later. However the rumour mill was now in full operation and we were aware that something significant was happening.

The few German troops in Meddersheim were mainly the guards for our work gang. They were ordered to retreat and to take we prisoners with them. It appeared that our liberation would be a little later than we had hoped. The thirty of us in our work gang were ordered to change from our work clothes into our military uniforms, and to pack our meagre belongings. Together with our guards, we then headed off in the direction of the Rhine. I suppose the farmers had been informed that all of their workers had been relocated when we failed to arrive for work.

It turned out to be an all day march. We shared the roads with thousands of refugees fleeing the upcoming battles as well as retreating troops who were on their way to prepare for those battles. The troops had right of way. As they approached, we prisoners and the refugees had to leave the road to give them clear passage. The military cars, trucks and armoured vehicles would not slow down or stop for anyone or anything. For most of the way, we were under the observation of spotter planes and occasionally fighters would also appear overhead. There was no German air force to speak of, so the Americans and British ruled the skies. Thankfully, they were not attacking anything on the roads, particularly with all the refugees clogging those roads. I am sure though that if their planes were fired upon, or if they came across any tanks or heavy artillery, their position would have quickly changed from observe to attack.

We skirted the city of Coblenz and, a few kilometers beyond the city, arrived at a barge river crossing on the banks of the Rhine. We were taken into a forest beside the crossing to rest and wait for further orders. Inside the forest, we came across some units of German troops already there resting up and waiting for their opportunity to cross the river. Our crossing was to be by barge during the night. The barge could not be used in daylight for fear of attack. It would have been defenseless out on the river.

Most of the bridges across the Rhine had been destroyed either by allied bombing raids or by the Germans themselves. The few remaining bridges were being used to allow troops and equipment to cross. They were under frequent attack by the allied planes which were trying to trap the troops on the south side of the river for encirclement by the Americans. The poor refugees had to find their own way across, or risk using one of the bridges.

While we waited, we rested as best we could. When our turn came, we were led down to the river and ordered onto the barge with our guards. The barge was basically a large pontoon that was pulled across the river by submerged chains. It easily held all the prisoners, our guards and a small crew. The crossing took fifteen to twenty minutes and went without incident. The barges could not be seen from the air at night and the American ground forces were still too far back to launch any form of assault or bombardment on the site being used for the crossing. Once we disembarked on the other side we were taken aside on the riverbank and led to an area that seemed to be a park. Once there, we were again told to wait.

The barge provided a constant stream of troops arriving at the riverbank. These troops marched off as soon as they disembarked. We prisoners just sat and watched the comings and goings. They did not want us to become mixed up with the troops or to be in their way. The troops had to be moved away quickly so that they would be some distance away by first light. The allied planes would certainly resume their observations and searches for targets as soon as the pilots could see. The Germans certainly did not want their crossing point or their barge to be found and attacked.

While we waited on the riverbank, we were each given a hunk of raw meat in an old food can. It was horsemeat. We had come across quite a few dead animals along the route and it appears that someone had gone to the trouble to butcher some carcasses for food. It was not something we could eat right away, but we had not eaten during the previous twenty-four hours and were very hungry. The meat would be cooked at the first opportunity. This opportunity arrived when the guards decided that it was unlikely that we would move off for a while. The guards allowed us to gather firewood and provided the matches with which to light our fires. We each put a little water into the cans with our meat and placed them onto the burning embers to slowly cook. Every so often, we would poke the meat to see if it was softening up and reaching the point where it was edible. The more I poked the meat and turned it, the harder that piece of meat seemed to become.

We were not destined, however, to eat our meat, either hard or soft. While we were cooking the meat, a fighter plane flew over our area. At this time, we were not unduly worried because this was not the first allied plane to fly over our group in the last few days and we had not been attacked. Surely, the pilot could see by our uniforms, as tatty as they were then, that we were not Germans. For whatever reason, the fighter suddenly swooped down and strafed an area very close to us. As it descended it also dropped two or three small bombs and then climbed away. At the first warning of the attack, we dived to the ground. As the fighter rose, we took off and ran in order to make ourselves difficult targets should the pilot decide to come back. Unfortunately, one of the prisoners had his leg injured by a bullet from the plane's machine guns. Once the plane flew off, the Guards bandaged his wounds and arranged for him to be evacuated to a hospital, probably in Wiesbaden. We quickly decided that would not go back to complete the cooking or to eat what may have remained of our meal.

Our flight to safety took us near a little village close to the river crossing. Once the guards had rounded up the rest of the prisoners, we walked the short distance into the town. The town had been partly destroyed, not by bombing or other warlike activity, but by looters. They had looted anything and everything from the shops, stolen what they could from the houses and left a trail of destruction in their wake. This is something that none of us or our guards had seen or come across before.

We continued through the town and stopped a short distance on the other side, where we left the road and sat down in an open field. It was an opportunity for a "breather" and a time to let our nerves settle after everything that had happened during the previous hour. All the German troops, apart from our guards, quickly left the area where the river crossing took place. Our group was now the only group left in the area.

Unbeknown to us, the American ground forces were not very far away. They had already crossed the river downstream from where we had crossed, and were following the course of the river. They were steadily approaching the position where we were resting. There was still a lot of aerial activity overhead but thankfully the planes did not bother with our group as we sat there in an exposed field. We had already received our breakfast ration of bullets and bombs for the day.

Then, in the distance we saw some soldiers heading in our direction across the fields. At first they were only small figures and we could not identify them. As they approached, we saw that they appeared to be American infantry soldiers, in what I guess would have been about company strength. Our guards must have been aware that there were American soldiers in the area because they seemed to be waiting for their arrival. As they neared our position, the soldiers immediately put down their weapons and raised their arms up into the air. We must have been quite a sight to the advancing Americans. Here was a group of men jumping up and down and cheering, while these soldiers just stood there with their arms raised. Once the Americans came up to us, the German guard Commander formally surrendered. He and the other guards were taken away, presumably to a prisoner holding point nearby.

The realization that we had been liberated was yet to come. When you have waited so long for something, as we all had, when it finally comes you want to taste it and savour it. Freedom is such a strange sensation when you have lived without it for five and a half years. The feelings I had at that time are extremely difficult to describe.

You cannot imagine our surprise and euphoria when some of the American soldiers came up and spoke to us in Polish. Others came and spoke in German. We were able to readily communicate with them. We had been liberated by a force of Americans, some of whom were descendants of our own countrymen who had previously emigrated to America, as well as Poles who had escaped to America before the war began and enlisted in the American army when war broke out. We all had a common goal, to defeat the Nazis.

We were taken back to the looted town and told to wait there. The Americans had arranged for some transport to come and evacuate us to a safe area. Before the American soldiers moved on, they gave us cigarettes, chocolates and lollies to tide us over until we could get some proper food. To the Americans such "goodies" may have been giveaways and part of their ration packs, but they were truly appreciated by us as they were not items that we had been able to get as prisoners. For the first time in a long time, I was again able to indulge my sweet tooth.

A large army vehicle arrived some two hours later. We were loaded on board and, with our little escort, headed off towards the city of Wiesbaden. The city was now in American hands. I am not sure how long we drove for, but time seemed to pass quite quickly. It did not feel like long at all before we arrived at our destination. We had been taken to a large military barracks some distance outside the city. I presume that the barracks had been taken over after the retreat of the Germans. There were many former prisoners, mainly Poles, already there when we arrived. There were also some civilians who had been released from Nazi internment. The numbers of liberated prisoners continued to grow as more and more men were repatriated from the Stalags and work gangs in our area.

At last, we were being taken care of extremely well. We had clean beds in which to sleep, sufficient food and the freedom to do whatever we wanted. We were not expected to work so our time was our own, to rest and to recharge our batteries. Many of the men circulated throughout the barracks looking for friends and acquaintances and, in some cases, family members. If they could not find them, they were after any information as to whether they were alive or dead or their possible whereabouts. I managed to find a few friends but, just as importantly, I made some new ones at the same time.

After a few days of the good life, we were assembled for an address by a senior American Officer. This officer spoke to us in Polish and informed us that the allies were forming a Polish Brigade to be attached to the British 8th Army. His mission was to seek volunteers to join this brigade, particularly from experienced combat soldiers. This was my opportunity, and I am sure the opportunity for many others, to seek our revenge on the Nazis and their allies. Many of us roared our willingness to volunteer and take up the fight again. The attack on our homeland had to be avenged and the perpetrators and criminals brought to justice.

Some of the men decided that they had had enough of war and its consequences, so they decided that they would not volunteer. We all understood that such a decision showed its own courage and these men were not seen as cowards or in any way as lesser men. There were others who reached the point of tears from frustration because they wanted to volunteer to resume the fight but were in no physical or mental condition to do so.

The next few days was taken up with administrative work, filling out forms and the like, as well as undergoing medical examinations to ensure that we were fit enough to continue with what lay ahead. I was fortunately deemed fit and joined the new brigade.

15

The Polish Brigade

Towards the end of March 1945, the volunteers were informed that they were being sent to join their new brigade. For the first leg of our journey, military truck transports arrived and drove us to the town of Joinville in France. It was a ten hour road trip and was rather poorly organised. There was no food or water carried on the trucks, and any requests for a stop to buy some food or to stretch our legs was refused. We were all very pleased to finally reach Joinville as it had turned out to be a long and arduous journey. We were to be billeted there overnight and for most of the following day.

The second leg of our journey was in a troop train, to the city of Clermont-Ferrand. In the evening, we left our billets and marched down to the railway station to begin the longest leg of the journey. This trip took twenty-four hours to complete and was far better organised than our previous trip. This time the train stopped at various towns for meal breaks and provided us with the opportunity to get off and stretch our legs. The train was quite full, but not to the point that anyone needed to climb up into the overhead luggage racks. On arrival at Clermont-Ferrand, we disembarked and were led to a military barracks located in the outskirts of that city. The barracks was already home to many hundreds of other volunteers who had opted to join the Polish Brigade. Our trainload simply added to the swell of people.

It was evening and we were all tired from the trip, so our first priority was to have something to eat and then to turn in for the night. The business of wandering around the camp and looking for relatives and friends was something that would have to wait until tomorrow. The next morning, the first item on the army's agenda was the issue of British military uniforms to all new arrivals. The uniform was the same as that worn by the British soldiers, but we were required to also wear an armband with "Poland" printed on it. This armband would identify us as members of the Polish Brigade and, just as importantly, provide us with a sense of our own identity. I was now a member of the 3rd Company, 2nd Corps, 7th Division, British 8th Army. Our Brigade Commander was General Anders, who was also a Pole.

After dressing in my new uniform, I spent the rest of the day roaming the grounds of the camp and wandering through the barracks and buildings. I was delighted to meet up with some old friends and acquaintances. It was good to know that they were alive and would be joining me in what lay ahead. My greatest surprise, however, was yet to come. That evening, as I entered the mess hall for dinner, I caught sight of some men with whom I had formed solid friendships while we were in Guttenberg. These men were members of the work gang from which I had escaped. They did not recognise me at first, until I was almost amongst them. The man who had been my closest friend in Guttenberg turned and looked at me, with surprise showing all over his face. He then asked whether I had a brother who had escaped from a work gang and been killed while escaping. I replied "Stasiek, are you blind? It's me, Zygmunt!" We hugged each other and the others then joined in our joyous reunion. Everyone was hugging each other and there were more than a few tears shed that evening.

Stasiek told me that the guards who had been with their work gang had told them that I had been recaptured and executed. They had said that that was the penalty for trying to escape. He also told me that the guard who had tried to kill me was transferred away shortly after, but they were not told where. Over our meal, I told them about what had happened to me, my actions in going into the military headquarters, my meeting with the German Officer and subsequent transfer to another work gang.

We remained in the Clermont-Ferrand barracks for three days. During this time, we were issued with new weapons and equipment and we spent many hours familiarizing ourselves with their effective use. It had been years since I last held a weapon of war in my hands. Once our training had been completed, our new Brigade was almost ready to return to the war. We did not have long to wait before we were heading for Italy.

16

Italy

Our easy life in Clermont-Ferrand was coming to an end. Once we had completed our retraining, we boarded a troop train and set off for the port city of Marseille. The train took us directly to the docks, where we boarded a troop ship to begin our voyage through the Mediterranean Sea. We had been assured that the Germans no longer had a navy, or much of an air force, left in the Mediterranean area of operations. The British did not expect any attacks, so our troop ship sailed unescorted both at sea and in the air. The only cause for concern was mines. The Germans had laid mines along access routes, so care had to be taken to avoid this danger. We began the voyage early in the morning and finally reached our destination, the Italian port of Taranto, late into the night.

Fortunately, our voyage was uneventful. The weather had been kind, so there were relatively few cases of men suffering from sea-sickness, although we were all very tired. We were able to get some sleep on the train leg, but very few of us slept on the sea leg. Our ship was alone out in the middle of the sea, and despite all the assurances regarding possible dangers, there was still a war going on. As soon as we had docked in

Taranto, we disembarked directly into troop transports that were awaiting us. The transports quickly took us to a camp that had been established some 20 kms away from Taranto in the town of San Basilio. This town was the base camp for the entire British 8th Army.

The next morning, we were granted two days of rest and recreation. After all our travelling, we certainly needed a break. A group of us decided to return to Taranto for a spot of sightseeing. The military had set up a system of transport to and from the city and it was well patronized during those two days. We were able to wander around and see the sights of the city and its harbour. Most of us did not have much money, so shopping and drinking were out of the question. The weather continued to be fine and warm and was ideal for our wanderings. Some of our group, myself included, took a swim in the sparkling blue waters of the Mediterranean. Despite the warm weather, the water temperature was still markedly cool, which rather restricted our swimming. There were also other soldiers, and sailors of many nationalities, who were sightseeing, just as we were. Unfortunately, few spoke Polish or German, so we could not easily communicate with each other. The local people of Taranto, however, were quite friendly towards us.

The two days of rest and convalescence proved to be a bonus. I was able to get rid of some niggling injuries and other aches and pains that I had been living with for some weeks. I was feeling very fit and well.

One of the facilities at the camp was a large outdoor movie theatre. The theatre operated nightly and was well attended for screenings of films, both new and old. The army in which we now found ourselves was so much different to what the Polish Army had been. Along with movies, they also screened newsreels, as well as military films on health & hygiene and general announcements to the troops. In fact, the evening after our arrival at the camp, we were assembled at the theatre to watch a short film welcoming the Polish Brigade into the 8Th Army and the camp at San Basilio.

Once our rest and recuperation period ended, we had to get back to the business at hand. The brigade was assembled for an address by its Commander, General Anders. He informed us that we were soon going into action at a place called Monte Cassino. Most of us had not heard of the place until that time. He told us that it was a monastery on top of a high mountain, and that it had been turned into a fortress by the Germans. This fortress had already withstood many allied attacks and bombardments. Due to its position, it dominated the high ground and the Germans could see the whole valley, including the roads and passes through the mountains. That road network was the only way to reach Rome. The Germans could see what was moving and where, and they were able to shell any of the roads or passes. Allied forces were being held up as they could not advance northwards on the road to Rome until the German's advantage was neutralised.

It was planned that our brigade, together with some of the British battalions, would attack and take the monastery and drive the Germans from the mountaintop. General Anders was passionate in his speech. He pointed out that this was our chance to strike a major blow against the Nazis, while at the same time showing the rest of the allied world just what we Polish soldiers could achieve.

17

Monte Cassino

The Army units that were to participate in the actual attack on the monastery and those units supporting the attack, were required to deploy to Monte Cassino. This deployment was achieved over three legs. The first leg was to travel by troop transports to Naples, 400 kms to our north. Throughout the day, troop transports began arriving at the camp. As evening fell, we boarded and the convoy set off on its first leg. For security purposes, it was decided that the convoy would travel through the night rather than in daylight hours. There was still some danger of German planes spotting and attacking our column. There were also pockets of Germans who had neither surrendered nor been captured, and even armed collaborators, roaming out in the countryside. They would be only too happy to mount an ambush on a transport convoy.

We reached Naples just before the sun rose the following morning. We had not encountered any problems during the journey. So far, the roads were reasonable and in good condition so most of us had been able to get some sleep, albeit sitting up, during the night. In Naples, we were billeted in an old palace that had been set up for our use. There were facilities for sleeping and washing, and we also had our own kitchen. The rest of the day was then our own. While some men slept, I and many others went into Naples on a sightseeing expedition. The weather continued to be fine and warm and we all enjoyed our time of leisure.

The second leg of our journey commenced that evening. This leg took us to the small town of Cassino at the base of the mountain on which Monte Cassino stands. From here, we would begin the third and final leg of the journey. Before leaving Naples, it was time to begin making preparations for going to war. This required the checking of our weapons, our ammunition and also our equipment to ensure that we had no nasty surprises at the worst possible moment. At the appointed time, we boarded the troop transports and the convoy started off. Again our journey had to be at night. We knew that the closer we got to Monte Cassino, the higher were our chances of being attacked by the Germans. They dominated the high ground and, from the monastery, could bring accurate artillery barrages onto our convoy. It was of prime importance to reduce our chances of being spotted and identified. The risks we faced in the first leg were only a trifling compared to the risks we now faced.

The road to Cassino was in a poor state and became worse as we approached the foothills of the mountains. There had been little road maintenance for some time and the road was littered with rubbish and junk that had been thrown away or left behind. Once in the foothills, the road became quite narrow and more winding. In some places, the road gradients were extremely steep. The condition of the road surface and the steep grades slowed the column down to a crawl. In other places the road had been cut out from the side of a mountain so there were drops of several hundred feet for any vehicles driven off the road. At one particular point the gradient was so steep that the troop transports could not go up in forward gear. The troops had to get off the vehicle and walk, while it turned around and reversed up the slope. At the top, the transport turned around again, the troops then boarded again and continued the journey. Eventually, although it seemed like forever, we reached the small town. However, our journey had not yet ended.

It was not yet dawn when we commenced the third leg from Cassino, the ascent of the mountain, towards our staging positions near the top. The mountain slope was steep and there were few tracks that we could follow in the darkness. The rest of the hillside was covered with jagged rocks and boulders and bits of vegetation. This combination of the terrain and the darkness made movement up the slope very difficult and somewhat hazardous. There were the ever present dangers of dislodging loose rocks onto the men following behind and of soldiers losing their balance and sliding down the slope themselves.

To add to our difficulties, we all had to carry our own extra rations and ammunition for the battle ahead. On top of that, we also had to somehow take with us additional stores, equipment and ammunition. Win or lose, we would be up the hill for a number of days, so all this was necessary. To assist with this task, the military had provided a number of donkeys. The poor beasts carried most of the additional weight, but despite this their gait was often more sure-footed than our own.

The sun rose while we were still clawing our way

up the mountainside. The first daylight provided us with our first clear sight of the monastery of Monte Cassino. The sight was truly awesome. We knew that it had been shelled and bombed many times and that it had already been assaulted by ground troops more than once. Yet, there it stood in all its majesty. From a distance, it seemed hardly damaged at all. We continued our ascent until we reached our staging point. Here, we were shielded from view from above and our positions were generally out of observational view from the monastery. From this position we would launch the final attack. The British troops had also completed their ascent and were settling down as well. The troops who were there awaiting our arrival gladly packed up and descended the mountain back into the town. The ascent had been difficult, but there were no major casualties among us, only some scrapes and bruises and a few broken bones.

I am sure that the Germans were aware of our arrival. It was likely that the arrival of a large convoy of troop transports had been reported to them, and surely they must have heard us climbing the slopes during the night. Once the sun rose, they may have had a clear view of some of our men from time to time. We needed to set up our defensive perimeter and establish patrols to dominate the surrounding area. This would hopefully discourage the Germans from counter-attacking or from interfering in our activities. Patrolling was paramount, particularly during the night.

There was one final hurdle that had to be overcome before we were able to attack. The Germans had laid anti-personnel mines over all access routes to the monastery. These mines had to be removed, or at least identified and marked, before we could venture into these areas. The sappers could only work at night to avoid being shot by snipers from the monastery. Each night, teams of sappers and protection patrols would go out into "No-man's Land", with the mission to locate and remove the mines. Many mines were removed and disarmed. In cases where it was too difficult or dangerous to touch the mines, their positions were marked with white ribbons. The defenders in the monastery must have suspected that an attack was imminent with all the nightly activity in "No-man's Land" and markers of white ribbon appearing here and there.

The mine clearing lasted two nights. Once finished, it was then a matter of us waiting to receive our orders before commencing our attack.

18

Attack on the Monastery

The order to begin the attack was received early the following morning. The attack was in the form of a pincer, with the Polish Brigade separating from the main body and attacking one side of the monastery. A British Brigade would also separate and attack the other side simultaneously. Once a break through had been achieved, the main body would advance and support the two pincers.

The 1st Battalion of the Polish Brigade led the attack from our side. The 2nd and 3rd Battalions, in company strength, advanced after them. The British were mounting their own similar maneuvre from the other side. The 1st Battalion persisted with their attack throughout the rest of the day. Squads of men were moving from any area of cover available to the next area of cover, locating and destroying the machine gun nests and any stubborn defenders in their holes and hideaways. The cost in casualties was high to both sides.

As night fell, my battalion moved up into the forward positions that were held by the 1st Battalion. They had up until then created and bore the brunt of the attack and it was time for us to take over. The 1st Battalion were being withdrawn to regroup and form our reserve. The fighting raged throughout the rest of the night. Most of the fighting was at close quarters and often hand-to-hand. In the darkness we could not see our attackers and they could not see us, until we were right on top of them. At times it was difficult to tell friend from foe. The noise of battle, exploding grenades, weapons firing and men screaming and yelling, continued unabated.

As dawn broke, the noise and battle began to subside. The German defenders began to surrender. First there was one surrender, then another, then a few more and then many more. They were raising white flags and crawling out of their foxholes and standing with their hands in the air, just waiting. The final push was nothing when compared to the fury of the previous day, and we were surprised with the relatively small number of prisoners that were taken. We learned that most of the defenders had pulled out and retreated during the night. Nevertheless, Monte Cassino was finally ours and General Anders had attained the goal he had so desperately wanted.

As we reached the entrance to the monastery, we were somewhat astounded to be welcomed by a monk. The British soldiers had not yet reached the entrance, so we Poles were the first to enter. While we secured the monastery and searched for any other defenders, a group of Polish soldiers entered the monastery and raised the Polish flag above the ruins. General Anders had been so confident of his brigade's victory that he had arranged for some soldiers to carry the Polish flag into battle with them and raise it as a symbol of victory for Poland and her people.

The flag fluttered proudly but did not remain aloft for long. One of the first actions of the British troops once they entered the monastery was to haul down our flag and hoist the Union Jack in its place. We protested and many of us were angered by their action. It would not have taken much more provocation for the Poles and Brits to have had their own battle. The standoff became intolerable and the situation remained tense while the matter was referred to Division Headquarters. A little later the Union Jack was lowered and, to the delight of the Poles, the Polish flag was again hoisted.

In hindsight, the battle had been a bloodbath. There were over a thousand Poles and Brits killed and many more wounded. I do not know what the German casualties were. From what I could see, I now doubt that the battle had been necessary. We found that the German defenders were out of food, low on ammunition and in general, a tired and totally dispirited lot. We could have gone around them and they would have eventually surrendered without the need for so many to die and suffer.

The memories of Monte Cassino still bring tears to my eyes. I will always see in my mind the incredible carnage, the blood and the destruction. Some of the brave men who had been in the forefront of the fighting broke down once the full picture unveiled itself in the cold light of day. Many others were physically sick. I was terribly saddened by the loss of life.

There is another memory that I have from all this. I realised that the mountain was covered in red poppies, wild flowers that grow abundantly in that area. The poppies were obviously there before the battle, but I had not noticed or paid any particular attention to them. It was not until I was looking for something positive from all that had happened there that I realised how beautiful the mountain looked. Being a Pole, I knew nothing of Gallipoli or the significance of the red poppy until many years later.

Without any fanfare we were ordered to return to the town of Cassino for a rest and some hot food. Once we arrived there, most of our men just laid down and fell into a deep dreamless sleep. For many, the nightmares were something that would come later, and many would be affected for the rest of their lives. The next morning, after breakfast, the troop transports returned and we were on our way back to Naples.

I do not recall much about our return journey to Naples. Most of us just sat in the rear of the trucks deep in our own thoughts. There was not much to be said to anyone as we had all been involved and had all seen the same things. Unbeknown to us at that time, Monte Cassino was to be our last battle of the war.

19

My Fighting is Over

We did very little over the next few weeks. Training slowed down and all the tasks we had to do were done with only as much urgency as was absolutely necessary. The war in Italy was now just about over and the allied troops were now moving up and threatening the core of Germany itself from the south and the west. Our communist allies were hewing a path of brutal death and destruction from the north and the east. The Polish Brigade was not to continue to play an active part in the war. We were now relegated to be occupation troops stationed in Italy.

I was granted a months furlough and decided to spend that time in Rome. Rome was a city that I had learned about in school and so I was anxious to see the Vatican, the Colloseum and the old Roman ruins. As a young boy, born and raised in Zwola, I could never have imagined having the opportunity to visit such places. In fact, I could never have imagined what would happen to me and how my life would be in 1945. Now here I was, in Rome, walking through the Vatican, praying in St Peters Basilica, winding my way through the catacombs and visiting so many other interesting places. It was the perfect opportunity for me to improve my Italian. I was slowly learning the language and now had the opportunity to practice it as well. My language skills improved in leaps and bounds to the point where to this day, I can easily make myself readily understood. The month of leave quickly passed and I then returned to military life in Naples.

For most of the time, I was stationed in and around Naples. However, there were still ample opportunities for day trips to places like Capri and Pompeii. Most of us grasped these opportunities whenever they presented themselves. As an occupation force we were often used to deliver and distribute supplies over much of Italy. We would also be used as peace-keepers in some areas where there was fighting within the local population. The fascists would be fighting the communists, and both would be fighting the resistance forces. For these operations, we would usually relocate into the area and remain there for several days - or longer if that was considered necessary. These operations provided more opportunities to explore and see other parts of Italy.

Unfortunately, at that time I was struck down with malaria and spent about 3 weeks in the Naples Hospital. Malaria is a particularly debilitating disease and I thought at the time that I was going to die. By today's standards the hospital was extremely poor and the medicines for diseases such as malaria were extremely crude. I managed to overcome the disease but it took its toll, and it was some time before I could say that I felt well again. Malaria is a disease that cannot be totally eradicated from the body, so I have also had the occasional relapse every now and then. Fortunately, these relapses are not of the same severity as the initial onset of the disease.

At the end of 1946, we were ordered to pack up our belongings. We were going to England. At the time when this order was received, we were temporarily stationed in Milan (Milano) and so our repatriation would begin from there. It was not long before we commenced the journey, initially by train. The train took us from Milan through Germany and then through France to the English Channel. The train trip, lasting several days, was far more pleasant than the previous train trips that I had been forced to experienced in those two countries.

We embarked on a troop ship and sailed for England, finally disembarking at Dover. The channel crossing was quite smooth and we were all delighted to see the high white cliffs while we were still some way out into the channel. None of us had ever seen such a spectacle before. After disembarking from the ship, we received an order to hand in our weapons. The war was over now, so there was no longer any reason why we should continue to bear arms. We found ourselves on a wharf, in a country we did not know, and with people who spoke a language that few of us could understand.

Our journey was still not over. Several hours after landing on English soil, we boarded a train bound for a place called Barrow-In-Furness. It was a long trip through the English countryside, passing through villages that were very different to the villages in our part of Europe. Some of the cities we passed through showed evidence of the devastation caused by consistent bombings throughout the war.

On arriving in Barrow-In-Furness, we were marched 3 kms outside the town to a camp in a small town called Daneghill. This was to be our home and base for operations until we were told what the future held for us.

The war was over for England, France and other parts of Europe. However, Poland was not free. The Poles had fought the Germans and the Russian Communists, firstly on their own and then her soldiers fought and died side-by-side with other allied soldiers. Poland was subsequently crushed by Stalin and his troops who claimed that they had come as liberators. Liberators, who together with the Germans, had actually invaded Poland in the first place and then divided the country between themselves. The only reason that they left was because they were routed by the Germans as part of Hitler's attack on Russia itself. The communist army was back and had taken control over the whole of Poland. The communists were back and they had no intentions of leaving. My beloved country was to suffer for many years before being able to throw off the yoke of communism.

The time came for an announcement about our future. Our commanding officer informed us that our brigade was to be disbanded. He only confirmed what we were already thinking, but it was still not easy to accept that we were no longer wanted as a fighting force. Our options were to stay and settle in England, return to our homes in Poland, or to emigrate to another country that was accepting émigrés and refugees. I made my decision quite quickly. I was not getting any younger, and I hated the thought of living under communist rule. The only thing that could have persuaded me to return was my family in Poland. However, not returning to them was a sacrifice that I felt I had to make, so I signed the resettlement forms to remain in England and became a British citizen.

Many others also chose this option. The men who did return had their own reasons, such as wives and children or careers. Sadly, they were not welcomed by the new communist authorities and many ended up in prisons in either Russia or Siberia. Few returned from this inhumane treatment. They just vanished from the face of the earth.

20

My New Life

To begin a new life meant that I once again had to become responsible for myself. I had to find work so that I could pay my way, but to get a job meant that I would need to learn the English language. As a POW in Germany I learnt German, and in Italy I also learnt their language, mostly by mixing with the Italian people as often as I could. So far I had only picked up a rudimentary knowledge of English but I decided that one more language would not be too hard to learn.

One night, a friend and I decided to go to a dance. Dances and live music were an important means of entertainment and a part of everyone's life in those times. We walked into town and the dance was already in progress when we got there. We walked inside, stopped and looked around. This was the first dance we had attended in England. I noticed two nice young women sitting near the wall, one wearing an army uniform. Not being one to stand around, I walked over to them and, in the little bit of English I knew, asked the girl in uniform for a dance.

I am not sure what she thought at the time but she

accepted my dance invitation. While we were dancing, I was trying to make conversation and asked her if she was a soldier. She looked at me and replied something about being a Scot. From this reply, I thought that she may have been a Scottish girl, but told myself that it did not matter if she was a Scot, as she looked like a nice girl anyway. She told me her name was Gladys. Some time later I found out that Gladys thought I was being "funny" by asking if she was a soldier, when I could clearly see that she was in uniform. Her actual reply was, "No, I'm Scotch Mist", but due to my limited vocabulary I misunderstood what she had said. That was in February 1947.

We danced together for most of the evening. As the dance finished late I asked if I could escort her and her friend (who was actually her younger sister) home. When we got there, she introduced me to her mother and I was invited in for a cup of tea and some cake. From that time on, we met quite often. Gladys was on extended leave from the army because of heavy snow around her camp. With her help, my English was improving every day.

One month after we met, on 28th March 1947, we became engaged and then on the 28th of June, three months later, we were married. To cover the costs of getting married, I borrowed eight pounds from the army NAFI. Gladys' brother Bill, who was serving in the navy but on leave at the time, gave her away. We were married in a little Catholic Church in a small village called Avon-Dasset, which was near Gladys' camp. We both wore our military uniforms for the special occasion. After the ceremony we drove to the town of Lemington Spa, where we had our reception.

There were five of us in the wedding party and the reception was held in a small café. We could not afford much but we still enjoyed strawberries and cream with tea or coffee. Our honeymoon was spent at Gladys' mother's home in Barrow-In-Furness.

The next thing for us to do was to obtain discharges from the army and to get ourselves civilian work so that we could begin our married life. We both managed to get jobs at a textile mill in a town called Rochdale, 120 kms away from Barrow-In-Furness. This meant that we had to leave the security and support we enjoyed with Gladys' mother and the rest of the family. We managed to find some accommodation quite near the mill. The accommodation was quite spartan, but it was all that we could afford at that time. I was to serve an apprenticeship as a mechanic at the mill and my wage was one pound fifteen shillings a week. Gladys was employed as a card tender and her wage was double mine at three pounds a week. To improve our lot, I began studying at night school to learn the methods being used to produce better cotton yarns. This education, together with my willingness to work hard and study, eventually helped me to get a job as a foreman in another mill in Rochdale.

We were fortunate that once we could afford more, we met a young woman who owned some cottages in Rochdale. She was in the process of selling them off one by one and so for the princely sum of fifty pounds we purchased one of the cottages. It was small and consisted of only two rooms, one up and one down, but it was our first home. We could not afford to pay the full purchase price in cash, so the woman accepted a deposit of five pounds, with payments of one pound per week until the remainder was paid off. There was no interest charged. The cottage was rather neglected so we spent quite a few late evenings and nights cleaning it up and redecorating. Once we had finished, we sold the cottage for two hundred pounds and earned ourselves a handsome profit. With this money we purchased a more modern house from the same woman. This time, our two hundred pounds purchased us a house with four rooms, two up and two down.

On the 5th November 1950, our first child, a daughter, was born. Eleanor Eugenia (Lena) was born early, but was a welcome little darling to us. After Eleanor's arrival, Gladys became a full time mum looking after our little girl. Over the next few years we had three more children, another daughter, Alexandra, and two boys, Stefan and Gerard. Tragically none of them survived, although Stefan managed to live for a day or so. We consulted a number of local doctors and a specialist in Manchester, but none of them could explain to us why our three children had not lived. To compound our anguish, they also suggested that any further children would most likely not survive either. They suggested that we would have to be content with our one darling daughter.

During Gerard's birth I almost lost my Gladys as well. She died during childbirth and was clinically dead for some minutes before they were able to revive her. Although they had managed to get her heart beating again, Gladys remained unconscious and then lapsed into a coma. Nothing the doctors tried was able to bring her out of the coma and she was admitted into the hospital. The doctors were pessimistic about her chances of survival, to the point where she had been given the "Last Rites". I sat with Gladys for as long and as often as I could but there was still Eleanor to care for. On the third day after the birth, I met the local priest in the hospital. We went into Gladys' room, knelt down beside her bed and began to pray. While we were praying she suddenly opened her eyes and looked at me. Then she said to me that she was sorry that Gerard did not live, but that everything was all right because he was now with my mother. I did not comprehend what Gladys was telling me at that time. I was just overjoyed that she had at last come out of the coma, recognised me and spoken. I called the nurses and the medical professionals then took over, providing the ongoing care and attention that was needed.

Once Gladys had recovered a little, she explained what she had meant about my mother. My mother had died some years earlier in Poland and Gladys had never seen her, not even a photograph. Gladys was able to fully recall what had happened to her during and after Gerard's birth. She remembered having gotten up from the bed just after Gerard was born and walking over to the trolley where he lay. She remembered picking him up and cradling him in her arms. He was alive and she was able to hold him close to her. While standing there holding him, she could also see herself still lying on the bed. She watched everything that the doctor and nurses did, and heard everything they said once they realised that she was on the edge of death. Then, suddenly that scene changed. The hospital activities seemed to become irrelevant and before her was a path that seemed to be in a sort of tunnel. This tunnel did not have any apparent or solid walls, it was more like a feeling that the path was surrounded by something. At the end of this tunnel was a vividly bright light. Strangely, this intense light did not blind her nor startle her. She knew instinctively that she and Gerard had to go down this path towards the light. Carrying Gerard, she stepped into this tunnel and walked until she had to stop once she reached a picket fence. The fence had a gate but it was closed and behind it stood a woman that Gladys instantly knew to be my mother. My mother extended her arms over the fence and told Gladys to give Gerard to her. Although no words were actually spoken, they could understand each other. After Gladys had passed Gerard over, she tried to open the gate and follow them. My mother told her that she could not go with them. She had to go back to take care of her Zygmunt and Eleanor.

The next thing Gladys remembered was waking up and seeing me kneeling beside her bed. She couldn't understand that three days had passed since the birth. To her, everything she had described to me had just occurred. Somehow, three days had been erased from her life. After she had recovered a little, she amazed her doctor and the nurses by describing to them what they had said and done during those minutes when she and Gerard stood by her bed and watched them trying to save her life.

Our lives were slowly improving. I was now earning higher wages and I worked overtime and on weekends whenever I could. We lived in Rochdale for some fifteen years altogether and in that time we bought and sold a few more houses. Each house we bought was better than the one before. With all the work that Gladys and I had done on renovations, we made a tidy profit on each house when we sold them. Our last home in Rochdale was in fact a building that contained a shop with living quarters above. I continued to work in the mill while Gladys shared her time in running the shop, a milk bar, and taking care of Eleanor. I suspect that her job was probably harder than mine.

It was not long before Eleanor's health began to take a turn for the worse. No matter how much we tried to protect her by keeping her warm and away from draughts, she was continually coming down with colds, coughs and sneezes. These infections were causing some deterioration to her lungs as well as damage to her chest. It became evident that the cold and damp Lancashire climate was not suitable for our Eleanor. Eventually, after a number of tests and examinations, we were referred to a specialist in Manchester. We consulted the specialist in June 1961 and, after a thorough examination, he told us that if we wanted Eleanor to survive another winter we would have to move to a warmer climate.

Australia House was situated not far from the specialist's rooms. We decided that, as we needed to move, perhaps we should move to Australia. It was a lot further away than the south of England or anywhere in Europe, but we had heard that Australia had a warm and dry climate. We simply walked into Australia House and applied for migration to Australia. Our application was accepted within a matter of weeks, and so in August we became "Ten Pound Poms". We sold up everything that we could and sailed from Southampton on a P&O ship called the Fair Sky. The voyage took four weeks, sailing over both calm and rough seas, before arriving in Fremantle. This was our first sighting of Australia. We were allowed to disembark from the ship and spend the day in the city. We could now see for ourselves what life in Australia was like and it was vastly different to life in England. Many of the buildings, particularly the shops and houses, had verandas that reminded us of buildings we had seen in American wild-west movies. It was nothing like what could be found throughout England and it only showed us how little we knew of our new homeland.

From Fremantle we sailed on to Melbourne which we had designated as our home port. We disembarked at Station Pier in Port Melbourne and were then transported to our first "Aussie" home, a migrant hostel in Brooklyn. There we were accommodated in Nissan huts, which were rather like army barracks. Unfortunately the hostel was located near a factory that often released some rather foul odours into the air. These odours made everyone's stay very uncomfortable and in fact affected the appetites of many of the hostel residents. Fortunately, we didn't need stay there for very long. I quickly managed to get a job at Preston Mills, a woolen mill in Footscray. While working there I met another ex-pat Pole named John Bigot. As luck would have it, John was looking for tenants to share his house in Ardeer. We moved in with him and lived there for about a year before we found and bought our own house in St Albans. It didn't take long to realize that the weather in Mebourne was much more suitable for

Eleanor and her health problems seemed to disappear quite quickly.

While working at Preston Mills, I took up a part time job as an agent with a real estate company called Wilmore and Randall. It was a large company that was involved with the development and sale of residential land all over Victoria. I worked with them during the evenings and on weekends. Once I had learnt the real estate trade and was confident that I could make a good living as an agent, I left Preston Mills to work in real estate full time. I remained in that industry until I finally retired at the age of sixty-seven.

With Eleanor at school, Gladys was able to hold a few part time jobs. Then she became pregnant for the fifth time, which came as quite a shock and concerned us greatly. We had been told by the specialist in England that it was highly unlikely that any further children would survive. We did not want to go through the anguish and trauma of losing another baby, having lost three already. We were referred to the Royal Woman's Hospital in Carlton, where the doctors conducted a series of tests on both Gladys and me. They were trying to determine what could have caused the deaths of the other babies. What they found was that Gladys developed diabetes whenever she became pregnant. However, the diabetes was not evident at any other times. They decided that, in order to increase the baby's chances of survival, Gladys would be admitted to hospital for the final twelve weeks of her pregnancy. These precautions were successful and in due course we had another beautiful daughter, Jeannette Ann (Jeannie).

We managed to give both our girls opportunities

for the education they wanted. Lena was married in October 1968 to Jerry Sanders (formally Jerzy Sawczuk). Jerry was born to Polish parents in Germany just after the war. As fate would have it we both fought in wars, Jerry in Vietnam and I in WWII. We were both injured, Jerry with shrapnel to the head and myself with a bayonet in the hand. I thank God that our injuries were not more serious. We are very proud of our son-in-law. He is a good husband and father. Lena and Jerry have given us three wonderful grandchildren, Lee, Lynda and Jennifer, who in turn have given us three great grandchildren, Georgia and Campbell (Lee & Kelli), and Lili (Jennifer & Anthony Siketa).

In 1971, we made a trip to the country where I was born, Poland. Our younger daughter Jeannie came with us. I had not been back to my former homeland from the time my battalion crossed the border into Hungary, more than thirty years earlier. We could not have received a more heartfelt welcome from my father, my sisters and brothers and the rest of the family. We then travelled on to England to see Gladys' mother and the rest of her family. We also took the opportunity to visit some of our old friends and neighbours whilst we were there.

In 1974, two members of my own family were able to come to Australia for a holiday. My younger brother Henryk and sister-in-law Wacia came for three months. They both enjoyed their stay and saw for themselves the differences between living in a country like Australia and a country under communist rule. They marveled at what Australia was and what it had to offer its people. Since then we have made a number of trips to Poland and England as well as a trip around the world. Sadly, both my father and Gladys' mother, as well as a number of our brothers and sisters, have now gone. This world is a poorer place without them.

Gladys is a very talented poet. She has written a little book of poems about our family, our overseas trips and special events in our lives. There have been many times when she has woken up in the morning and told me that she has a lot of words cruising about in her head. She would get a pen and paper and within just a few minutes would be reading a beautiful poem to me. I have included a poem that Gladys recently wrote at the end of my story. It was written for our diamond wedding anniversary (60 years) and was beautifully read by Tori, our fourth grandchild, at our anniversary celebrations.

In 1985, Jeannie married James Joughin. They were married in the chapel at Carey Grammar the school where James was educated. That same year Jeannie graduated from Monash University with a Bachelor degree in science. Later she graduated with a PhD. She worked in the Alfred Hospital and then accepted an offer to finish her post-graduate studies in Innsbruck, Austria. When her studies were completed, Jeannie returned home and began work at Bristol Squibb. She has worked for a few companies in Melbourne and is now a Director of Marketing for CSL in Parkville, travelling all over the world with her work. In January 1995, her first daughter Victoria (Tori) was born. Twenty months later her second daughter, Emma, our fifth grandchild, was born. They are both beautiful young ladies and are a credit to their mother.

Since I retired from work, Gladys and I chose to live in Daylesford and to take care of each other for the rest of our lives. We enjoy a large circle of friends here and have found all that we need to keep us happy and comfortable. We still get about in our trusty little car and from time to time take bus trips. I am a member of the local bowling club, playing both pennant bowls and social games. I am still fit enough to take care of our garden and grow some vegetables for our table. We are always happy to see our family, either here in Daylesford or at their homes.

Gladys and I have now been married for over sixty years and we plan to be around a bit longer. We have just had a wonderful anniversary celebration that began with an overnight stay in a city hotel. We were picked up and chauffer-driven to and from the hotel. We then had a celebratory lunch with family and friends the following day, which I am sure everyone thoroughly enjoyed.. Both of my daughters worked hard to ensure that our celebrations were a success. They arranged for us to receive congratulatory letters from the Queen, the Prime Minister, the Governor General, and the Governor of Victoria, as well as some other politicians. Both Gladys and I are deeply touched by everything our family has done for us.

In closing my story, I have to say that I am now more than ninety-three years old and I have had a fortunate life. There have been some tragedies at different times as well as some tragic years, mostly during the war. I have lived through these and am now enjoying a happy and contented life. My health is still good and I plan to be around for some time yet. I want to say to everyone in my present and future family to be happy and to love and respect each other. May the Good Lord bless you all!

AS LONG AS TIME REMAINS

Where would I have been?
What would I have done?
If you had not been by my side
For I was just a girl
When you took me for your bride.

As the years rolled gently by
You've been my mentor and my friend
And now I know
Our love will never end.

We've had our worries and our woes
As people always do
But we held on tight together
And we came smiling through.

Our children brought us so much joy
As we watched them grow
And now we have our grandchildren
And great grandchildren too
Who will fill our hearts with happiness
As children always do.

And as we walk
Still hand in hand

THIS SOLDIER'S FORTUNE

We turn to each other and smile
For we know we have been blessed
To be together for that while.

Sixty years have gone so fast
And if I lived them once again
There's nothing that I would change
For we will always love each other
As long as time remains.

Gladys Tratkiewicz 2007

A word of thanks

I would like to thank my son-in-law Jerry for the assistance he gave me in writing this story. His own experiences have enabled him to be able to help me to find the words that I needed.

THIS SOLDIER'S FORTUNE

THE TRIALS AND TRIUMPHS OF A POLISH SOLDIER IN WWII

www.ingramcontent.com/pod-product-compliance
Lightning Source LLC
Chambersburg PA
CBHW070554160426
43199CB00014B/2503